Artists of the Tundra and the Sea

ARTISTS OF
THE TUNDRA
AND THE SEA

By Dorothy Jean Ray

University of Washington Press

SEATTLE AND LONDON

Copyright © 1961, 1980 by Dorothy Jean Ray
First paperback edition, with corrections, 1980
Second printing, 1984

Library of Congress Cataloging in Publication Data

Ray, Dorothy Jean.
  Artists of the tundra and the sea.

  Bibliography: p.
  Includes index.
  1. Eskimos—Alaska—Sculpture. 2. Ivories.
I. Title
E99.E7R25 1980 736'.62'09798 79-27420
ISBN 0-295-95732-8

Printed in the United States of America

Introduction to the 1980 Edition

A QUARTER of a century has passed since I spent a summer with the ivory carvers in Nome and studied the Eskimo ivory collections of American museums for this account of contemporary ivory carving in northern Alaska. Without a break in the long tradition of ivory craftsmanship, another generation now supplies collectors, tourists, and museums with carvings, many of which are as good as, if not better than, those of twenty-five years ago.

Of the men whom I photographed in King Island Village in 1955, only Aloysius Pikonganna is living, still a supreme carver at a youthful seventy years of age. Many of the old carvers' sons are also carvers, but others, like Francis Pikonganna, Peter Seeganna (who died in 1974 at age 36), and Bernard Katexac, have entered the world of fine arts with their silversmithing, wood sculpture, and printmaking.

In 1955, ivory carving in all of western Alaska—including Point Hope and Wales in the north and on Nunivak Island and in the Yukon-Kuskokwim area in the south—was oriented toward the souvenir market. The term "Eskimo artist" was used either as a special designation for artists working with what was considered to be atypical media for an "Eskimo"— for example, oils and canvas by Howard Rock (Weyahok) or ink and reindeer skin by George Ahgupuk—or else as a blanket term for the incredibly large percentage of the population that derived all or part of its income from ivory carving. At that time, all arts and crafts had an ethnic orientation, and it was important that both artist and subject matter be "Eskimo."

This can no longer be said after twenty-five years. Photographs of recent work in many media in my *Eskimo Art: Tradition and Innovation in North Alaska* (Seattle: University of Washington Press, 1977), as well as in other publications mentioned at the end of this introduction, illustrate the changes that have taken place. During the past fifteen years especially, the

Eskimos of Alaska have been given opportunities for formal art study almost undreamed of in 1955: the Designer-Craftsman Training Project of the Manpower Development and Training Act in 1964-65; inauguration of the Extension Center for Arts and Crafts at the University of Alaska in 1965; the Village Art Upgrade programs and other community projects made possible by state and federal funds, and visiting artists programs in the public schools in the 1970s; and establishment of the Visual Arts Center of Alaska in Anchorage in 1972.

With the exception of a few attempts by local persons to teach Eskimo children to carve and sew in the Bureau of Indian Affairs schools, the only formal arts and crafts project attempted in western Alaska before 1955 was the Shungnak jade project in 1952. At that time, ivory carving *was* "Eskimo art" to the buying public despite Ahgupuk's and Rock's works, the production of baleen baskets in Barrow and Wainwright, a few fur dolls here and there, or the trickle of masks made by the Nunivak Island and other southwest Alaska woodcarvers. Even in southwest Alaska, where the few available ivory carvings rarely made their way to metropolitan markets, the best-known endeavors were also ivory—the unique "Nunivak tusks" of the middle decades of the twentieth century (figs. 68-74).

It is somewhat disconcerting to realize that most of the artists who have taken advantage of formal art training, and whose works in various media are now eagerly sought, were only boys or teen-agers in 1955: Lawrence Ahvakana, Sylvester Ayek, Earl Mayac, Teddy Mayac, Melvin Olanna, John Penatac, Francis Pikonganna, Harvey Pootoogooluk, Michael Pullock, Peter Seeganna, Joseph Senungetuk, Ronald Senungetuk, John Tingook, Justin Tiulana, Clifford Weyiouanna, and many others.

There have been other changes since the 1950s. More women carve now, and more carvers use power tools, although most of the work is still done with hand tools. Some of the surface effects of new carvings are achieved only with power tools.

The King Islanders moved permanently from their island home to Nome in 1967, but they are still among the foremost ivory carvers of Alaska. The supply of walrus ivory has not dwindled, but raw ivory is very expensive—possibly from ten to fifteen times higher than in 1955—for those who do not hunt walrus as do the Little Diomede Island and St. Lawrence Island people. But the carved ivory is just as costly. One of Aloysius Pikonganna's bears (fig. 64) would now cost from twenty to thirty times the 1955 price of $12.50. (In Anchorage in 1979, I saw an ivory bear somewhat larger than this one, carved by a woman with power tools for a shaggy fur effect, which was priced at $650.00.) This expense, as well as an increasing recognition of ivory carving as a desirable art form, has led to the signing of many pieces. Ivory carving is no longer an anonymous art.

Neither do the carvers struggle along on an average income of $900 a year, as in 1955, and though almost unlimited employment opportunities for both men and women have opened since then, the ranks of the ivory carvers do not seem to have thinned. The King Island carvers do not work in a community house, as in 1955 (figs. 5, 6, 94, 95), but at home, many of them in a new housing project built in Nome after they had abandoned their island. The final desertion of King Island Village east of Nome, however, took place on 12 November 1974 when a destructive storm leveled almost all of the buildings.

The airline tours that began in the early 1950s to Nome and Kotzebue (page 12) have developed into a tourist industry of sizable dimensions. Eskimo people of Kotzebue are especially enthusiastic participants in the daily festivities during the tourist season. The routines and some of the participants are the same as I observed in 1961—the venerable Paul Green, Helen Seveck, and Chester Seveck. There are, of course, some differences. They now dance and sell their souvenirs in the formidable museum of the NANA (Northwest Alaska Native Association) Regional Corporation's huge multipurpose building, instead of in a room in the old Wien Air Alaska's hotel, and the audience can now sit on bleachers that disappear with the touch of a switch instead of sitting on old wooden chairs. The routines of dancing, anecdotes, and selling are done against the background of a commercial visual and auditory package, the dances being introduced by a dramatic voice on tape and by slides and graphics blown up to gargantuan size on a screen above the stage. And, after the dances, Mr. Seveck now brings out a stack of his popular booklet, *The Longest Reindeer Herder*, first published in 1973, to sell along with the slippers and ivory carvings.

The most obvious changes in Eskimo art have taken place in media other than ivory—painting, metal work, lapidary, printmaking, stone sculpture—but as demonstrated in both *Artists of the Tundra and the Sea* and *Eskimo Art*, styles in ivory are constantly changing. Since 1955, fewer cribbage boards, billiken figurines, and necklaces have been produced. Bracelets of all kinds, however, have continued in popularity. More human figurines are now made, some depicting traditional costumes, some engaged in typical activities, and some as female nudes. Mythical creatures, which were engraved on drill bows and walrus tusks during the nineteenth century have become popular as three-dimensional sculpture, and animals that have usually been thought of as "Eskimo"—whales, seals, and walrus—are now interpreted in more variable styles and poses. The stocky, sturdy figurines of all kinds no longer have the market to themselves, and delicate, breakable figurines have become quite popular, although the dogs of the dogteam bracelet are still made in low profile so they will not snag on clothing. Group sculpture has become more abundant, and almost every activity has been tried: dancing, blanket tossing, fishing, seal hunting, and whaling.

A recent trend among the northern carvers has been the borrowing of southwest Alaska motifs and forms. A foremost example of this is the ivory "mask," a form that was originated by a Nunivak Island man in the 1950s. A delicate and beautiful one made by King Islander John Kokuluk, which I bought in Nome in 1979, has a central "mask" of a human face inside an eagle's beak (which was not a northern style), with eight radiating appendages of small ivory masks in both King Island and Yukon River style. Thus, he had borrowed both new and old forms.

The first borrowing of a southern design by the northerners can be traced to the Kivalina caribou hoof project, which was inaugurated in 1956 by the Indian Arts and Crafts Board. Frank Long, the arts and crafts specialist in charge of the project, introduced a Kuskokwim mask style of the 1880s as a jewelry design (see *Eskimo Art*, fig. 187, which is similar to fig. 87 in this book). Subsequently, ivory carvers have copied other designs from various publications on Eskimo art.

Since the success of the Canadian soapstone sculpture, which was in its infancy at the time I wrote *Artists of the Tundra and the Sea*, Alaskan ivory carvers and "Eskimo artists" have glutted the Alaskan market with copies or their own interpretations of this sculpture. Occasionally there is an excellent piece—even a masterpiece—but the majority rarely attain the heights of mediocrity of the worst of ivory carvings.

During the passage of twenty-five years it is inevitable that books and articles about Eskimos would be written. By 1955, comparatively little had been written about Eskimo art, and although the bibliography to this book might more appropriately have been titled, "References Used," the list would not have been appreciably longer had I listed everything pertaining to Eskimo art. Since 1961, the date of this publication, there has been a veritable flood of articles, books, and catalogs pertaining to Eskimo art. A complete list is out of the question here, but a fairly comprehensive survey can be acquired from the following selected publications and their reference or bibliography sections.

In 1967, the entire autumn issue of *The Beaver* was devoted to Eskimo art of Alaska, Canada, and Greenland. Especially useful are the bibliography and two articles: "A Retrospective Glance at Canadian Eskimo Carving" by Charles A. Martijn (pages 5-19), and "Prehistoric Dorset Art" by William E. Taylor, Jr., an archeologist, and George Swinton, an artist (pages 32-47).

Before 1961 only a few pamphlets had been written about the developments of the then-new Canadian soapstone sculpture, and the ones that I had read were really not an honest appraisal of the art, but rather an idealistic fairy tale treatment. George Swinton has put this art in perspective in two well-documented and illustrated books, *Eskimo Sculpture* (Toronto, Montreal: McClelland and Stewart, 1965) and *Sculpture of the Eskimo* (Toronto: McClelland and Stewart, 1972). The latter contains an extensive bibliography of Eskimo art, archeology, and ethnology.

Also relating to Canadian Eskimo art is a chapter, "Eskimo Art: The Eastern Canadian Arctic," by Nelson H. H. Graburn, in a collection of essays, *Ethnic and Tourist Arts* (Berkeley: University of California Press, 1976), edited by Graburn. The introduction to the book, entitled "Arts of the Fourth World," is a provocative discussion of the arts of native peoples who have been "subject to internal colonialism." An article, "The Historic Period in Canadian Eskimo Art," by Jean Blodgett in the summer 1979 issue of *The Beaver*, discusses and illustrates some hitherto unpublished souvenir objects from the Canadian Arctic.

The literature on Alaskan Eskimo art has increased almost as much as that of Canada. I have written on the specific subjects of graphic arts and masks: "Graphic Arts of the Alaskan Eskimo" (whole issue of *Native American Arts* 2, Washington, D.C.: Indian Arts and Crafts Board, 1969) and *Eskimo Masks: Art and Ceremony* (in collaboration with Alfred A. Blaker, Seattle: University of Washington Press, 1967). General discussions and illustrations of the entire spectrum of Alaskan Eskimo art can be found in my *Eskimo Art* and *Aleut and Eskimo Art: Tradition and Innovation in South Alaska* (Seattle and London: University of Washington Press, 1980); and in a long article by Saradell Ard Frederick, "Alaskan Eskimo Art Today" (*The Alaska Journal*, vol. 2, no. 4, 1972, pp. 30-41).

Although not directly concerned with Eskimo art, three general books are useful for background material of archeological periods and art styles: *Ancient Men of the Arctic* by J. Louis Giddings (New York: Alfred A.

Knopf, 1967); *Alaskan Eskimos* by Wendell H. Oswalt (San Francisco: Chandler Publishing Company, 1967); and *The Eskimos and Aleuts* by Don E. Dumond (London: Thames and Hudson, 1977). Numerous examples of extraordinary Okvik and Old Bering Sea objects, found in Siberia, are illustrated by S. A. Arutiunov and D. A. Sergeev in *Drevnie Kul'tury Aziatskikh Eskimosov* (1969) and in *Problemy Etnicheskoi Istorii Beringomor'ia* (1975), both issued by Akademiia Nauk SSSR, Moscow.

Since the publication of V. V. Antropova's long paper on Chukchi and Eskimo art in 1953 (page 124), another well-illustrated monograph, *Chukotskaia, Koriakskaia, Eskimosskaia, Aleutiskaia Reznaia Kost'*, was written by E. P. Orlova (Novosibirsk: Akademiia Nauk SSSR, 1964). She illustrates several billikens, which were originally created by a Kansas City, Missouri woman in 1908, but which have now been firmly entrenched in the folklore of Siberia—so much so that the billiken was the subject of a paper by anthropologist N. N. Dikov in 1973, "O Proiskhozhdenii Pelikenov," in *Zapiski Chukotskogo Kraevedcheskogo Muzeia* (Magadan, vol. 6, pp. 15-19). In 1974, I also brought the history of the billiken up-to-date in an illustrated article, "The Billiken," in *The Alaska Journal* (vol. 4, no. 1, pp. 25-31).

The comparatively meager bibliography on the Yankee whalers' scrimshaw, was augmented in 1972 by a comprehensive volume, copiously illustrated, *Scrimshaw and Scrimshanders*, by E. Norman Flayderman (New Milford, Conn.: N. Flayderman and Co., Inc.).

Since 1961, many museums have issued catalogs of their collections or of special exhibits, which included Eskimo arts and artifacts. Representative of such publications are *Alaska State Museum Bicentennial Catalog*, compiled and edited by Bette Hulbert (Anchorage: Northern Printing, 1976); *A Catalogue of the Ethnological Collections in the Sheldon Jackson Museum*, by the museum personnel (Sitka, 1976); *Eskimo Art in the British Museum*, edited by William Fagg (London: British Museum, 1972); *Die Eskimo*, catalog of the Eskimo collection of the Staatliches Museum für Völkerkunde, Munich, by Otto Zerries, with the assistance of Jean-Loup Rousselot (1979); *Survival: Life and Art of the Alaskan Eskimo* by Barbara Lipton, with an annotated bibliography by Allan Chapman (Newark, N. J.: The Newark Museum, 1977); *The Far North* (Washington, D.C.: National Gallery of Art, 1973), especially valuable for its many good illustrations; *Sacred Circles* by Ralph T. Coe (Kansas City, Missouri: Nelson Gallery of Art—Atkins Museum of Fine Arts, 1977); and *The Coming and Going of the Shaman: Eskimo Shamanism and Art*, catalogue of an exhibit at the Winnipeg Art Gallery, 1978, Jean Blodgett, curator of Eskimo art. *Contemporary Native Art of Alaska* is a catalogue of an exhibition at the Anchorage Historical and Fine Arts Museum in 1979.

Museum collections have also been the subject of monographs. Two that are most pertinent to the subject of northern ivory are *The Bruce Collection of Eskimo Material Culture from Port Clarence, Alaska* by James W. VanStone (*Fieldiana Anthropology,* vol. 67 [Chicago: Field Museum of Natural History, 1976]) and *Eskimos of Northwest Alaska in the Early Nineteenth Century* (based on the Beechey and Belcher collections) by John R. Bockstoce (Oxford: Pitt Rivers Museum, University of Oxford, 1977).

During the past two decades collectors of "primitive" art, and even of the fine arts, have come to appreciate the value of Eskimo art in their own collections. Consequently, in 1976, Sandra Barz began publishing a quarterly newsletter, *Arts and Culture of the North,* which provides worldwide information about Eskimo art for collectors and dealers, as well as museums, libraries, and scholars.

There are only a few additions or corrections to the text of *Artists of the Tundra and the Sea,* despite the march of time. Since 1955 I have learned that Guy Kakarook of St. Michael was also an excellent engraver of ivory tusks, which I had not known until I examined the collection at the Lowie Museum in Berkeley, California, where I found the same scenes engraved in ivory that he had painted on paper. He also apparently began making cribbage boards about the same time as Happy Jack (pages 18, 30). (I illustrated a number of Kakarook's water colors in "Kakarook, Eskimo Artist," in *The Alaska Journal,* vol. 1, 1971, pp. 8-15.)

As of 1955, no bow drill had been taken from an archeological site (page 23). In 1959, a whole drill bow was collected from a burial, supposedly of Thule age, near the Canadian village of Arctic Bay on northern Baffin Island. This mysterious bow, which is illustrated on page 8 of *The Beaver* art issue (1967), has not been joined so far by further archeological companions—not even in Alaska where drill bows had been collected by the hundreds from the early to the late nineteenth century.

By now it is fairly well established that all Okvik and Old Bering Sea engraving was done with metal tools as suggested on page 9. The objects from these archeological periods have become so popular and costly on the world art market since 1961 that the Eskimos themselves have dug up many figurines and other art objects on St. Lawrence and Punuk islands to sell.

I have come to the conclusion that the figurine illustrated in figures 37 and 38 was carved by or for—or represented the adventures of—a shaman named Asetchuk in Point Hope folklore, or some other shaman similarly talented in flying (see *Eskimo Art,* pages 120-21).

The spelling of Eskimo names in English has been a perennial problem. In this book I spelled Aloysius Pikonganna's name Pikongonna, which was sometimes used in official documents of the city of Nome. It is now always spelled Pikonganna, though pronouned, "Pikwana." The St. Lawrence Island name, Numayuk, can also be spelled Numaiyuk, and the village of Ayacheruk at Cape Nome can be spelled Ayasayuk in a different dialect.

Although the ivory carvings and ivory carvers of the post-gold rush days have now slipped into history, there is no end in sight to the durable tradition of making ivory objects. I wish that I could be here a hundred years hence to see what changes the Eskimo artist will have made. Perhaps the most noticeable changes will be in the greater use of non-native materials, subjects, and styles. Yet, as long as there are walrus, there will be ivory; and as long as there are walrus hunters there will be carvers.

Port Townsend, Washington
November 1979

Preface to the Original Edition

THIS story of the Alaskan Eskimo ivory carvers began in 1945 when I first lived in Nome. Between that time and 1950 I became acquainted with a number of carvers as I gradually acquired some of their work, but I did not then have the opportunity for the concentrated research necessary for a complete picture of this important part of Eskimo life.

In 1950 I made an economic and social study of Nome with a research grant from the Arctic Institute of North America. Because of the scope of the study, I obtained only a small amount of information about ivory carving, but this whetted my appetite for more, and so I returned in 1955 for a summer with the ivory carvers. I spent the majority of the time in Nome and the King Island Village to the east of it but fortunately was also able to make a brief trip on the *North Star*, the Bureau of Indian Affairs ship, to St. Lawrence Island.

I have also studied the major archeological and ethnological ivory collections in various museums for the purpose of adding visual substance and, sometimes, reinterpretation to the history of Eskimo art. Some of the photographs reproduced herein were taken at that time.

Numerous persons have offered help and information during the gathering of material for this publication. Margaret Lantis and Otto William Geist, both experts in Eskimo lore, have unselfishly given their encouragement and information. The directors and staffs of the various museums whose collections I photographed, without exception, gave me unlimited use of their facilities and, in spite of the disruption that is bound to occur, retained their interest and equanimity to the end.

I wish to thank in particular the following for their help in various capacities: at the American Museum of Natural History, New York: Harry L. Shapiro and James A. Ford; at the Historical Museum of

Mystic Seaport, Connecticut: Malcolm D. MacGregor and Louis Martel; at the Peabody Museum, Harvard University, Cambridge, Massachusetts: Gordon R. Willey and Bert Carter; at the United States National Museum, Washington, D.C.: Frank M. Setzler, H.W. Krieger, and R. A. Elder; at the University of Alaska Museum, College, Alaska: Ivar Skarland; and at the University Museum, University of Pennsylvania, Philadelphia: Froelich G. Rainey, Alfred Kidder II, Schuyler V. R. Cammann, J. L. Giddings, Jr., J. Alden Mason, and Henry N. Michael.

My special thanks go to Margaret Currier, the keeper of the magnificent anthropological library of Peabody Museum (Harvard), for her unfailing sense in the mysteries of bibliography. In this respect also, my thanks to Ronald J. Todd, Margaret McClure, Jessica Potter, Ruth M. Kirk, and Margaret Trudo for their cooperative and sometimes backbreaking work of supplying the printed word at the University of Washington Library.

My gratitude is endless for the hospitality and help given to me by three long-time residents of Nome, Mrs. Carrie McLain, Mrs. Earl Towner, and Mrs. Mike Willoya.

Lastly, I want to extend my appreciation to those carvers who by word and deed contributed to this book about themselves. In 1955 from King Island there were John Killarzoac, John Charles Oarlarana, Aloysius Pikongonna, and Thomas Samnarana. From Little Diomede Island, "Big Mike" Kazingnuk, "Spike" Milligrock, Bob Omiak, and Riley Ozenna. In Nome lived James Sirloak and George Washington (Soksrok), both formerly of King Island, and Andrew Tingook, formerly of Shishmaref. The St. Lawrence Island carvers who contributed were Louis Immingan, John Ipungalook, and Jerry Wongitillan.

I had known a number of the above-mentioned carvers in the 1940's as well as several others who had died in the meantime: Riley Ozenna's father, a master carver who had made his home for many years on the "Sandspit," west of Nome; and Jack Secco and his son, both formerly of Little Diomede Island.

All photographs, unless otherwise indicated, are mine.

DOROTHY JEAN RAY

Bothell, Washington

Contents

Figures

Artists of the Tundra and the Sea

ONE: Nome and Happy Jack

CONTEMPORARY Alaskan ivory carving appeared to blossom suddenly during the mad rush for gold in the Eskimo territory of Cape Nome at the turn of the century. But it cannot be dated from any specific year because the wheels of change already had begun to turn ever so slowly in that direction during the last half of the 1800's as traders trickled into the area and whalers wrought their changes on the fringes of the land. One event, however, stands out more clearly than the rest, mainly because it involved one of the best-known carvers of the contemporary scene, Angokwazhuk, or Happy Jack.

In 1892 a whaling ship skippered by Captain Hartson Bodfish put in at Little Diomede Island. The whalers had visited both Little and Big Diomede islands to buy fur products ever since their first journeys through Bering Strait in 1848. Sailors in that part of the world encountered extremely cold and bitter weather for the greater part of their trips, and the Eskimo parkas and mukluks protected them better than anything else. Furthermore, sometimes the geometric fur designs on the garments were so beautiful that they later were cherished as mementos of the trip.

Captain Bodfish did not expect his trip ashore on this visit to Little Diomede to be different from any other he had made to villages along the coast, and perhaps even after he had weighed anchor he had no reason to remember it as an important event. But his encounter may well stand as the real beginning of the contemporary ivory-carving industry in Alaska.

In accordance with customary procedure of trading in the nineteenth century, the Eskimos usually came aboard with their fur products, meat, fish, old tools, walrus ivory tusks, and often vast quantities of baleen, the popular "whalebone" used for women's corset stays. At certain places, and Little Diomede Island was one of them, they also brought small ivory carvings to trade or sell.

Ivory carving in this part of the world was nothing new. For almost two thousand years ancestors of the Bering Strait Eskimos had designed beautiful things of ivory. The years came and went, the designs changed, but always they were the products of great esthetic inspiration and technical skill.

On this occasion Bodfish learned that a young carver of unusual ability, Angokwazhuk, was unable to come aboard to trade his ivory. This news, alone, would not ordinarily have sent a sea captain ashore because there were a number of very good ivory carvers both on the islands and on the mainland of Bering Strait. But Bodfish had heard of Angokwazhuk's harrowing experiences of the previous winter and wanted to meet this youth who was not only a courageous man but a talented carver.

Angokwazhuk, only about nineteen years of age, and his hunting partner had come face to face with the worst when they had drifted on the ice pack of the Bering Sea for almost a month that winter before making their way back to shore. Angokwazhuk, already an experienced hunter at that time, had been the sole provider for his mother and younger sister. Although he was born near Ayacheruk, a village on the present Cape Nome, he had moved with his widowed mother to Big Diomede Island when an older sister married a man from there. Upon her death at twenty-one he had moved to Little Diomede, the home of his mother's relatives.

His partner died on that fateful hunting trip, but Angokwazhuk, more dead than alive, was able to drag himself back home. However, it soon became apparent that he had frozen his feet, which had to be amputated. He nearly lost consciousness before he could summon a man to perform the operation, and the story goes that Angokwazhuk, himself, bade him sharpen "three long knives" to cut off his toes and half of each foot near the ankle.

When Captain Bodfish entered the small stone building characteristic of the homes on the island, he found a slight and rather wistful youth lying on a built-up bench that served as a bed. In spite of the language barrier he immediately took a great liking to the good-natured boy. He was also greatly impressed by his ivory carvings, for although the ivory work of the Bering Strait Eskimos was known to be better than that of any other Eskimos in the world, this was marked by the stamp of genius. The exact reasons why Captain Bodfish offered to take Angokwazhuk on board ship and thence to San Francisco, his home port, are obscure, but it certainly must have been the combination of a real interest in the youth and in ivory carving, and the possibility of adding another seaman to his crew.

However, Angokwazhuk was adamant in his decision not to go on such a long and perilous journey. Like all Eskimos he had a deep love and passionate attachment for his bleak and monotonous homeland, and the thought of strangers and of leaving his own friends made his heart sink. He wanted to stay on his island in spite of the fact that from now on he would have no status as a hunter, the most important role in his culture. But a man who had heard the story from Happy Jack's own lips said that Bodfish extravagantly offered him "everything under the sun if he would go, so he went." That evidently put the cap on the argument, for Captain Bodfish shortly afterward set sail with Angokwazhuk aboard after the whole village had pushed him down the rocky, snowless slope of the island in a sled.

It was customary for whaling and expedition ships to hire Eskimo men and women as hunters, sailors, or seamstresses. Even today a few Eskimos can remember relatives or friends who had taken long journeys on ships before 1898, the year in which gold was discovered near Nome, when white men were rare in the northern part of Alaska. But this turned out to be quite different. Angokwazhuk evidently did nothing but carve during the entire trip, a pursuit every Eskimo man enjoyed. As for Happy Jack, it was like being in an ivory heaven.

On this trip he was successful both as a man and as a carver. The sailors gave him two things: first, the nickname of "Happy Jack," which became synonymous with exquisite ivory carving during the early days of Nome; and, second, many new carving ideas. These, when incorporated with his basic technical knowledge and unlimited talent for adaptation and revision, started contemporary ivory carving on the path which it still follows today.

The world had long known that the Eskimos of the Bering Strait region were artists in ivory. Fine examples of their work had trickled into the museums of the world ever since Captain Beechey had returned home in 1828 with an engraved piece of bone.[1] Both scientists affiliated with expeditions and whalers returned with quantities of the typically engraved scenes and small figurines of this area, and by the time Nordenskiöld called attention to the ivory carving in his book *The Voyage of the Vega* in 1882,[2] numerous persons already had discovered that the Eskimos were anything but icebound, untalented people.

The Eskimos' artistic output in the nineteenth century consisted primarily of graphic art, or two-dimensional sketches (Figs. 44-52), but they also made numerous small carvings in the round for utilitarian purposes such as drag handles or buttons (Fig. 35). Their engravings of this time appear to have been purely for pleasure, although a number of so-called "hunting tallies," with numerous animals, were in all probability hunting records.

Happy Jack, in setting the stage for present-day carving, deviated considerably from the older style by incorporating styles of scrimshaw art, that unusual art of the whalers, with his own technical proficiency. Some of his graphic interpretations were realistic and almost photographic in contrast to the more impressionistic ones of the earlier artists.

Despite his ominous forebodings, Happy Jack's first trip to San Francisco was so enjoyable that he later made another, although it is not known whether or not it was with Captain Bodfish. Carving on board ship had turned out to be both profitable and interesting, and since, once he had returned home, the market for his work was limited to passing ships, he was contemplating a third voyage when gold was discovered on Anvil Creek, only a few miles from his birthplace, Ayacheruk.

There is little doubt that it was this historical event which brought

[1]F. W. Beechey, *Narrative of a Voyage to the Pacific and Beering's Strait, 1825-1828* (London, 1831), Part I, p. 251; Part II, p. 573.

[2]A. E. Nordenskiöld, *The Voyage of the Vega round Asia and Europe* (New York: Macmillan and Co., 1882), pp. 577, 578.

the new style and concepts of Eskimo art into maturity in such a short time. Although Happy Jack remains in the memory of all, Eskimos and non-Eskimos alike, as the first and most important figure in ivory carving, a few other carvers from the Aleutian Islands to Point Barrow were dabbling in the same sort of thing. Until the Nome gold rush, however, there was no concentrated demand necessitating prodigious production by numerous carvers, and it is probable that, if it had not been for that event, the isolated attempts at the new style of carving would have developed into several regional ivory art styles instead of the basic one of today.

Happy Jack's arrival in Nome suddenly precipitated the famous carving market of the first decade of the 1900's, setting a pattern that has deviated little in the almost sixty years since it began. The most common items for sale in the first two or three years after the gold strike had been the Eskimos' own cultural commodities, fur products and tools in their old tradition: mukluks, dolls, mittens, and hoods; flint knives, arrowheads, ulus (women's knives), skin scrapers, bow drills, adzes, sled runners, and plain ivory tusks. Little carved ivory was peddled on the streets along with their native artifacts by the Eskimo men. When articles other than fur products were newly made, they were likely to be tools or needlecases. The latter, a typical Eskimo manufacture, which had been made in a variety of forms from Greenland to East Cape, Siberia, were the first ivory objects actually made expressly for the Nome tourist trade. One man in 1900-1 made nothing but souvenir needlecases of the same design, but they were copies of an old artifact, not carvings in the new tradition.

In spite of the fact that the discovery of gold sent thousands of persons to the beaches of Nome, the Eskimos were slow to come (Fig. 2). The present site of Nome had never been popular with the early inhabitants of Alaska because subsistence conditions were relatively poor. Within easy reach of Ayacheruk, the closest Eskimo village to Nome, ten miles away, there was to be found only small game, including rabbits, ptarmigan, ducks, geese, and, in the winter, tomcod and king crab caught through the ocean ice. The men had to travel considerable distances for caribou, oogruk (bearded seal), beluga (white whale), walrus, polar bear, and whale.

When the population of Nome had reached thirty thousand in 1900, it included only a handful of Eskimos. They pitched their tents on the

Sandspit to the west of town and earned a little money by selling game or their old tools. They were not hired to work in the mining operations in those first years because there were dozens of experienced persons from the United States and Europe competing for every available job.

After Happy Jack's arrival and his proven success in a new livelihood, a number of Eskimos came to stay. From the start his versatility and ingenuity were recognized, and his wares were in demand not only by those who wanted typical ivory carvings, but by those who wanted something made "by the famous Eskimo carver, Happy Jack."

His most notable achievement was the copying of photographs and halftone reproductions from magazines and newspapers to ivory (see Fig. 53). He reproduced faithfully every dot or hachure mark from the printed page so that his copy had the appearance of a photograph printed on the ivory itself. In many cases, the ivory picture was better than the original.

The first pieces that Happy Jack made and sold in Nome were, however, the cribbage boards formed of a whole ivory tusk (Figs. 54, 55). These were scrimshaw-inspired; for the cribbage board of wood or sperm whale tooth was one of the staple items of the whaling man's scrimshaw repertoire. Although a few ivory cribbage boards antedating Nome have turned up in museums, none evidently was made before 1892 when Happy Jack went on his first whaling voyage. When E. W. Nelson made his magnificent collection of ivory artifacts for the Smithsonian Institution from June, 1877, until June, 1881, he did not collect any cribbage boards.[3]

Although the carvers have always assumed that Happy Jack made the first walrus ivory cribbage board, it is possible that a trader or sailor had suggested the idea of a cribbage board to an unknown carver somewhere in the vastness of coastal Alaska at about the same time. However, it was Happy Jack's esthetic and competent treatment of these boards which made his name synonymous with them.

It was not long before his versatility came to the attention of the traders, and he continued to try out new ideas in carving until his death in the disastrous influenza epidemic of 1918. His willingness to try any-

[3]Edward William Nelson, *The Eskimo about Bering Strait* (Bureau of American Ethnology, Annual Report, Vol. XVIII, Part I, 1899).

thing suggested to him was an important element in his popularity. (See, for example, two items made at a customer's request in Figures 56 and 76.) Happy Jack was the first to recognize that ivory carving of the future was to be done for a different purpose and for a different culture from before. A new kind of art would supplant the Eskimos' utilitarian objects. Two factors contributed to this development: the realization, first, that their own ivory implements could be supplanted by very acceptable metal substitutes, and, second, that the esthetic drive hitherto realized mainly in utilitarian implements could be carried out in the new styles of sculpture.

It was not only Happy Jack's carving ability that set the stage so successfully in those early years, but also his personality. His nickname of Happy Jack was well chosen, for everyone recognized his optimistic and happy spirit, and some did not even suspect that his halting gait was the result of walking around on stumps of legs with the feet cut off. Without doubt one of the characteristics that has endeared him in the minds of his own people for so long was his unselfishness with his carving ideas, techniques, and tools. In other words, he was the ideal, and idealized, Eskimo man—completely selfless and cooperative, but with every reason to be the opposite. From the moment that he began to carve in Nome, his home was open to others. In fact, it has been pictured as a kind of school for carvers, with the men coming in the morning and often staying the entire day. They were free to use Happy Jack's ideas and his tools, which he had either invented or modified from foreign ones. He helped them with carving and technical problems and would even do some of a fledgling artist's work.

His home, on the Sandspit near the present cemetery, was not only a workshop but a social center. No one ever left his house hungry, although the carvers who ate meals there day after day usually helped to pay for them or brought food. Frequently their meals consisted of mutton, which Happy Jack could buy by the whole carcass for five dollars from a cold-storage plant in Nome.

His talents, moreover, did not end with carving. Having learned to play the accordion on board ship, he was particularly fond of acting as accompanist for the singing of hymns. On Saturdays he served the triple role of host, interpreter, and accompanist when the Seventh-Day Adventist missionary met with the Eskimos gathered together in his house.

Nome today is still the ivory-carving center of Alaska, and it still draws carvers from everywhere in the Bering Strait region. They use the basic principles, ideas, and tools of Happy Jack and his contemporaries, but demands for certain objects have come and gone. It is remarkable that after sixty years there are still superior carvers who, like Happy Jack, can take their place among the best. We shall see what factors contributed to this stability.

The present carving population of Nome consists both of Eskimos who have migrated from outlying villages to live in Nome permanently and of those from King and Diomede islands who come to Nome in their oomiaks (skin boats) for the summer, usually in time for the Fourth of July celebration. Scarcely a village from the northern half of coastal Alaska is not represented, although the majority are from Seward Peninsula. The migration of Eskimo families to Nome has increased steadily over the years. The Eskimo population probably represented less than 2 per cent of the gold rush inhabitants, but the percentage had more than doubled by 1903-4, when the total population had dropped to 3,185 in the winter and about 5,000 in the summer, the Eskimo numbers remaining essentially the same. In 1940, when the population was only 1,550, two out of three were of Eskimo background, while at the present time at least three-fourths of an estimated population of 2,000 are Eskimo or mixed bloods.

The greatest increase came during World War II when job opportunities unfolded for the Eskimos. They were given not only new kinds of jobs, but many of the existing ones which had previously been filled only by whites, who had left Alaska when invasion seemed imminent. In 1941 for the first time an Eskimo woman was hired for work other than domestic labor.

With an increasing use of Eskimo labor and a lessening of prejudice in Nome, there awakened at this time a sense of justice and fairness for the Eskimos as well as for other native peoples in Alaska. Up until this time in Nome, Eskimos or persons who looked like Eskimos were not allowed to eat in a restaurant or take a room in the hotel. They were segregated in the movie theater to the balcony and one side, and were thrown out if they attempted to sit on the "white" side. Only in the years immediately before the war did the Eskimos live anywhere but on the fringes of town, either on the far reaches of the Sandspit to the west, or near "King Island Village" to the east.

Racial equality, at least in outward appearance, was effected by the territorial legislature in February, 1945. Section 1 of chapter 2 of H.B. 14 reads:

> All citizens within the jurisdiction of the Territory of Alaska shall be entitled to the full and equal enjoyment of accommodations, advantages, facilities and privileges of public inns, restaurants, eating houses, hotels, soda fountains, soft drink parlors, taverns, roadhouses, barber shops, beauty parlors, bathrooms, resthouses, theaters, skating rinks, cafes, ice cream parlors, transportation companies, and all other conveyances and amusements subject only to the conditions and limitations established by law and applicable alike to all citizens.

The Eskimos of King and Diomede islands, for the main part, however, have refused to move permanently to Nome, although they have been asked repeatedly why they do not leave their islands, which are physically uninviting. They are completely isolated for about nine months of the year except for an annual visit by an icebreaker if the weather is favorable.

There are many reasons for their choice. The majority of the men have not learned a skill that could qualify them for full-time employment, and, even if they were qualified, it is doubtful whether there would be enough available jobs. The unskilled mining and longshoring jobs during the summer are already held by these men. Second, and most important, they do not want to leave their islands to live in Nome. They would rather risk a lean year of hunting than the uncertainties of employment and the extremely high cost of living in the city.

Knud Rasmussen noted in 1924 that when the Bureau of Education discussed the possibility of moving the King Islanders to St. Lawrence Island, where they would have better educational advantages, "the proposal was discussed, but the meeting quickly declared that no time for consideration was necessary; not a single family wished to leave that barren island, which they loved and regarded as the finest settlement in the whole world."[4]

Probably the most sensible objection is that "Nome is a hard place for us." Even the young men in their twenties say, "Nome isn't a good

[4]Knud Rasmussen, *The Western Alaska Eskimo,* posthumous notes edited by Erik Holtved and H. Ostermann (Report of the Fifth Thule Expedition, Vol. X, No. 3, 1952), p. 74.

place for us." The saloons are overfriendly, and the policemen are over-eager to nab a weaving Eskimo and part him from a sizable slice of his hard-earned money. It is a rare man who can subsist on the proceeds from carving when nine hundred dollars is considered a very large yearly income from that source, and actually no man can do it without supplementing his diet with a large amount of native food.

But they continue to come to Nome each summer where they live in a cluster of houses on the beach to the east of Nome known as King Island Village (Fig. 4). For over thirty years the King Islanders have resided in their wooden cabins in that area, while the people from Diomede Island[5] inhabited the Sandspit, across town in the opposite direction. Recently, however, a number of Diomeders have begun to pitch their tents among the wooden houses of the King Islanders, and some have even given up their Nome jaunt to go for the summer to Kotzebue, where, they say, the market for ivory carvings is better. This is partially true for a limited number of carvers because one of Alaska's airlines has inaugurated a package tour of flying, feasting, and fun in Kotzebue and Nome, with Kotzebue as the first stop. Here the carver grasps his opportunity to weaken the tourist's sales resistance before he lands in Nome. However, the summer bustle and the traditional visiting with old friends soon lure the carver back to Nome for at least another summer.

Until about 1947, the King Islanders carved under overturned oomiaks on the beach in front of their little village. At that time they acquired a number of wooden buildings from the Bureau of Indian Affairs for homes and turned one of them into a *kazgi* (men's house), where most of the carving is done. This is where the display table is located, and visitors are permitted to enter, watch the men carve, and look over the wares (Figs. 5, 6). Except for the fact that the sand and sea do not blow into the customer's eyes while he is purchasing an ivory bear, none of the romance is gone. They are the same Eskimos, the same carvings, and the same negotiations.

[5]In this account, Diomede Island is used interchangeably with Little Diomede Island, which is in the United States.

TWO: The Ancient Carvers

T HERE is no doubt that the carving of ivory into pleasing shapes has been carried on uninterruptedly from the earliest known Eskimo culture to the present. The high percentage of decorated tools and other objects in archeological sites reveals that artistic motivation has been an important thread running through the entire history of the Eskimo.

Increasing archeological discoveries have given a firm outline to northern Eskimo prehistory with undisputed evidence that the Eskimos had always been distinguished craftsmen and at times extraordinary artists. The Eskimos of the Bering Strait area worked with wood, bark, skins, and baleen ("whalebone," from the mouths of the Mystacoceti suborder of whales), but no material was so enduring for future appreciation, or evidently so satisfying to the artist, as the hard but workable ivory. Throughout these years the carver confined his talents to objects that were to be used, rather than merely looked at. Thus, everyday implements—harpoon heads, bag handles, and needlecases—were engraved with exquisite designs that exemplified a unity of form and decoration.

So far, little archeological art has been found south of Bering Strait in the southwest Eskimo territory. The art of this region seemed to appear suddenly in the nineteenth century although undoubtedly there are undiscovered archeological antecedents. One of the most interesting features of the nineteenth-century southwest art is its profuse geometric decoration of the sort which the northerners had discontinued several centuries before to turn their engraving talents to the depiction of realistic scenes. The earliest artists used engraving purely for ornamentation, but those of the Thule culture of about 1700 used it for the expression of a realistic idea. Their meager little sketches on ivory were the forerunners of the elaborately engraved pieces of the nineteenth century. It has been suggested that the early ornamentation might have had symbolic or ritualistic significance, but there is no way to determine that now.

The earliest Eskimo period known to date is called "Okvik," meaning "where walrus haul up," and has been discovered on St. Lawrence Island and at East Cape, Siberia. The St. Lawrence Island Okvik is thought to be two thousand years old, dating back just before the birth of Christ, and the Siberian Okvik is possibly a thousand years older.[1]

These ancient carvers were master engravers who covered their harpoon heads, cups, and strange, unidentified figures with fresh, spontaneous designs (Figs. 8-16, 108, 109). One of the striking features of the Okvik archeological collections is the preponderance of dolls, often without legs or arms, but with rather carefully made faces (Figs. 8-12). The lack of interest in the body suggests that they were to be covered with clothing, although, in one or two cases, a few incised lines resemble the delicate geometric fur trim of present-day parkas.

More attention was given to faces, which could not be camouflaged by clothing. Whether from Siberia or St. Lawrence Island, features of these faces are so diagnostic that an isolated head in a collection would be recognized immediately as belonging to an Okvik figurine. The faces and noses were unusually long, the chins narrow, the mouths small, and the eyebrows carefully incised. Sometimes tattoo marks were placed on the cheek or chin. This period produced one of the most beautifully sculptured figures in the entire history of Eskimo art, the "Okvik Madonna"[2] (Figs. 8, 9).

A larger percentage of implements was decorated at this time than at any other with the possible exception of the nineteenth century in

[1]Chester S. Chard, "Eskimo Archaeology in Siberia," *Southwestern Journal of Anthropology,* XI (1955), 168. There are conflicts in the dating of Okvik and Old Bering Sea. Use of the Carbon-14 technique of evaluating the age of objects may reveal Old Bering Sea to be older than Okvik with Punuk possibly contemporaneous with Old Bering Sea (Froelich G. Rainey and Elizabeth Ralph, "Radiocarbon Dating in the Arctic," *American Antiquity,* XXIV, No. 4 [1959], 367, 369).

[2]Another one similar to this was purchased on St. Lawrence Island in 1939, but the head had been broken off (Froelich G. Rainey, *Eskimo Prehistory: The Okvik Site on the Punuk Islands* [Anthropological Papers, American Museum of Natural History, Vol. XXXVII, Part IV, 1941], p. 522).

southwest Alaska. For instance, over one third, or 463, of a total of 1,125 bone and ivory specimens found at the Okvik site on Punuk Island were decorated.[3] Although they were profusely engraved, there was little in this style to foreshadow the realistic engravings of nineteenth-century Eskimo life, many centuries later, which were at one time the only Eskimo art known.[4] The few attempts of the Okvik artist to depict tattooing and decoration on clothing have no relationship to the realistic engravings in which action, time, and space are represented.

The Okvik artist seemed compelled to decorate even the simplest of his objects in such a spirit of breathlessness that it is as though he was in a hurry to get it done. The most used element was the spurred line, which can be made hurriedly but produces a highly decorative effect. Another speedy device was the making of short gashlike marks placed in a row or radiating from a central area.

Although succeeding art styles employed essentially the same single elements, it was the combination of the elements, the arrangement of them on an object, and the depth and width of the incisions that created entirely new impressions. Okvik art, in its more offhand use of these combinations, gives the feeling that the ivory was a vehicle for the artist's sudden inspiration, a testing ground for the combination of designs. Later Old Bering Sea art, however, presents the appearance of planning. The intricate designs in their perfection must have been tried over and over again in the artist's mind if not on some other medium before being perpetuated on the ivory.

Although Okvik has been recognized separately, some regard it as merely an early stage of another Eskimo culture known as Old Bering Sea.[5] There is, however, as much difference between the art motifs of Okvik and the late Old Bering Sea material as there is between Old Bering Sea and Punuk, which followed it. On the basis of design there is every reason to believe that the Okvik from Punuk Island and Siberia was contemporaneous with so-called Old Bering Sea I from the main-

[3]*Ibid*, p. 543.

[4]Walter James Hoffman, in his *The Graphic Art of the Eskimos* (U.S. National Museum, Annual Report for 1895, Washington, D.C., 1897), written before contemporary carving began, and before the archeological sites had been uncovered, treats these realistic engravings in detail.

[5]Henry B. Collins, Jr., "The Origin and Antiquity of the Eskimo," *Smithsonian Institution, Report 1950* (Washington, D.C.: Government Printing Office, 1951), p. 430; J. L. Giddings "The Archeology of Bering Strait," *Current Anthropology*, I, No. 2 (March, 1960), 123.

land of St. Lawrence Island, especially from the Hillside Site.[6] Actually there is little to distinguish them except color, those from Punuk Island usually being lighter. The paucity of Old Bering Sea I objects on St. Lawrence Island may mean that they were imports from Punuk Island.

Although the later Old Bering Sea engravers employed essentially the same simple motives as did those of Okvik, even to the combination of solid and broken lines, they used them to create very complex over-all designs in which the ellipses and circles often enclose a bosslike prominence (Figs. 17-22, 108, 109). This is especially true of the harpoon heads and some of the unidentified objects, which sometimes were covered with a succession of bosses, the encircling lines connected to broken or straight lines to form a balanced and sophisticated pattern. At other times the lightest touch of the Okvik and the heaviest of Old Bering Sea were combined, with circles, ellipses, and heartlike outlines drawn in a heavy line and repeated with a lighter one within each design, producing an effect reminiscent of the quilting stitches of a patchwork blanket. Probably no other Eskimo artists were more conscious of the relationship between design and form or were so successful in making them such close companions.

It is useless to speculate whether or not these engravings had symbolic or other special meaning, but an objective examination of some of these complicated designs reveals birdlike characteristics (Fig. 22). These are most readily seen in many of the late Bering Sea harpoon heads, in which the spurs of the harpoon head resemble the wings and the blade slot is so related to ellipses and circles that there is no mistaking the design of mouth and eyes.

Unlike the Okvik, the later Bering Sea designs were often engraved on large objects. The artist must have felt a need for expansion, carrying his complicated and intricate work to harpoon foreshafts and, in many cases, large unidentified objects.[7] The Old Bering Sea artist, using the same elements as preceding artists, differed from them by constructing more design zones and combining them to form a compact unit through careful repetition. These zones were emphasized through the use of two

[6]Henry B. Collins, Jr., *Archeology of St. Lawrence Island* (Smithsonian Miscellaneous Collections, Vol. XCVI, No. 1, 1937), p. 40.

[7]For examples see *ibid.*, Pls. 16, 18, Figs. 1, 2, 3, and 4; Collins, "The Origin and Antiquity of the Eskimo," Pls. 2d, 3b, 3d, and 3h; and Aleš Hrdlička, *Anthropological Survey in Alaska* (Bureau of American Ethnology, Annual Report 46, 1930), Pl. 19, Pl. 20, No. 12.

devices, one, the use of liplike eminences around a zone, and the other, a raised boss that created an inner climax to the design. Both of these altered the form of an object. Previous artists would have been content to create the design in only two dimensions by engraving on a flat surface, but the classic Old Bering Sea artist added a third dimension. These changes in the shape of the object emphasized the engraved curves and broken lines.

Uniquely related to Okvik and Old Bering Sea art is that of Ipiutak, a large village site near Point Hope (Figs. 29-32, 110, 111). It was once considered "pre-Eskimo," but has been dated as about nine hundred years old on the basis of radiocarbon examinations.[8] Larsen and Rainey suggest that these Eskimos arrived at Point Hope during the first or second century A.D., having previously lived in northern Siberia along the Ob and Yenesei rivers,[9] but this date may prove to be too early. Whatever its age or origin, this site is one of the most provocative yet found in the Arctic because of its lack of many "typical" Eskimo items, particularly sleds, bow drills, and harpoon floats, and because of its extraordinary art objects. Swivel and openwork twisted objects, the only ones of their kind found so far, were discovered in conjunction with Okvik and Old Bering Sea specimens. Gracefully "modern" in concept, the twisted double spirals often were attached to long bird heads with links of ivory. Although one of the favorite motifs of the Ipiutak Eskimo artist was the bird, there is no relationship between his style and that of Old Bering Sea. The former seemed to make them as realistic as possible in spite of his other abstractions, while the latter conventionalized them as if to capture and confine a flight of fancy into a mold of finite proportions. Only the head is emphasized in both cases, with the exception of the winglike resemblance in the spurs of Old Bering Sea harpoon heads.

Very little of the rich imaginative art of these three cultures remained subsequently in northern Alaska. By the eighteenth century the art had become simple and austere, and realistic both in sculpture and engraving (Figs. 33-36, 44-51, 83, 84). Fanciful and complicated concepts did not end in Alaskan territory, however; they appeared to be newly located

[8]Henry B. Collins, Jr., *Arctic Area—Indigenous Period* (Programa de historia de America)(Mexico City: Instituto panamericano de geografía e historia, 1954), p. 85.

[9]Helge Larsen and Froelich Rainey, *Ipiutak and the Arctic Whale Hunting Culture* (Anthropological Papers, American Museum of Natural History, Vol. XLII, 1948), p. 160.

in the southwest Eskimo area. By 1877, when E.W. Nelson began his famous collection of artifacts for the Smithsonian Institution, the southwest Alaska Eskimos were decorating ivory implements with multiple and complicated designs. Geometric ornamentation was restricted to the ivory, but the portrayal of imaginative and fantastic animals was also carried out in wooden articles, including masks (Figs. 41, 42, 43, 85-88). Until more archeological work is done in that region, there is little to suggest whether this art grew out of Punuk, Old Bering Sea, Ipiutak, or was a result of other influences. Probably it was a combination.

All of the three foregoing art styles—Okvik, Old Bering Sea, and Ipiutak—create the impression that the artists were expressing themselves more or less spontaneously. The Punuk period that followed these was characterized by a very different art style. The Punuk artists evolved a precise and disciplined art with a rigid use of the nucleated circle and the straight line (Figs. 23-27). Their art has sometimes been called degenerative because of its simplicity as compared with its predecessors, and stiff because of the clean and spacious use of simple elements.

Yet, strangely enough, essentially the same elements are used as in previous periods. Punuk art is not so ornate as late Old Bering Sea and is better planned than Okvik. The design is well balanced, and the thoughtful arrangements of a few slightly curved and straight lines on the length of all four planes of a harpoon head is as pleasing as the laciness of Okvik ornamentation or the ponderous ornateness of Old Bering Sea. The placement of the design is done with as much regard to the shape of the object as in the Old Bering Sea style but in a more uncluttered and linear manner. It is as if the Punuk artist was more concerned with directional spacing of elements than climax, and with creating space rather than seeking to fill it.

Collins has said that the art of Punuk was the product of metal tools and that the culture grew out of the preceding Old Bering Sea and new influences from Siberia.[10] He was led to this conclusion by the fact that no iron tools had been found in association with Okvik and Old Bering Sea artifacts, and by his belief that the deeper incisions and highly regimented character of elements in Punuk art could not have been done with chert, jade, or flint.

[10]Collins, "The Origin and Antiquity of the Eskimo," p. 429.

The depth of incisions should, however, be no criterion for the use of metal tools. Many modern Eskimo engravers deliberately make shallow and feathery marks with the finest and sharpest tools, while others bear down deeply into the ivory. Incisions that represent feathers on small birds today are sometimes so shallow that they barely can be detected with the fingernail. The present-day carvers insist that only the sharpest tools can produce such accurate and delicate incisions and that, because engraving demands that tools be better cared for, some of the laziest and most careless carvers do little of it today.

It is possible that Okvik and Old Bering Sea designs were also engraved with metal, for an iron-pointed engraving tool was found at Ipiutak where many objects indistinguishable from the Okvik and Old Bering Sea objects of St. Lawrence Island were excavated.[11] It should be noted that, although metal was in existence at Ipiutak, it was not the "stiff" Punuk art, supposed to be the result of using metal tools, that was found there. On the contrary, it was the "spontaneous art" that supposedly preceded metal tools.

It is historically possible that Okvik carvers could have used metal since iron was commonly used in eastern Asia by A.D. 300. It is more possible that the Old Bering Sea people used it since they supposedly were later, and their curvilinear and circular motifs would demand greater technical control, nor is the fact that they did not use compass-drawn circles any reason to believe that they did not use metal. Knowledge of metal does not necessarily include knowledge of a double-ended compass, and acquaintance with the compass does not necessarily mean preference in using it.

It is only when we approach the historical period of the 1800's that conclusions can be ventured. Even so, a great deal of the collected material lies in our museums without a clue to its exact provenience, and, except for an occasional reference, the artist's motivations and attitudes have gone to the grave with him.

This is the period that gave rise to the realistic engraving of scenes on ivory slabs, something unknown in the art styles already discussed. However, in an archeological site in central Canada, Naujan, T. Mathiassen in 1922 found seven fragments of ivory with simple pictographs, for

[11]Larsen and Rainey, *Ipiutak and the Arctic Whale Hunting Culture*, p. 159.

example, a caribou and an oomiak with a man in it.[12] The period represented by this site was named Thule, the first prehistoric Eskimo culture to be described systematically. Although this was before the archeological discoveries of Okvik, Old Bering Sea, and Ipiutak, it was a revelation because the consensus up to that time had been that the many etchings on ivory had been learned from Europeans, particularly the Russians who had settled Alaska first.[13] However, not only had these Eskimos not been in contact with the Russians, but the site appeared to be very old, probably dating from A.D. 1000.[14]

Then, in 1924, a few pieces very similar to those made by the Canadian Thule artists were found near Point Barrow, Alaska. However, this collection, obtained by Knud Rasmussen, was a hopeless tangle because it had been gathered haphazardly by both traders and Eskimos and contained both recently made and ancient pieces.[15] It was thought that even the older objects had been made since the eighteenth century and had possibly been brought back from Canada by a return migration of Thule people supposedly contemporaneous with the Punuk culture on St. Lawrence Island. In 1938, however, several pictographs were found near Cape Prince of Wales which appeared to be much older than those from Point Barrow and which might have been made by the Thule people before they went eastward and thence back again.[16]

Strangely enough, though many objects typical of Thule were found on St. Lawrence Island, there were no pictographs. The Thule people also were noted for making quantities of human and animal figurines as well as flocks of flat-bottomed birds, but these do not appear until a much later time (Figs. 28, 33). They were equally noted for the paucity

[12]These are illustrated in Therkel Mathiassen, *Archaeology of the Central Eskimos* (Report of the Fifth Thule Expedition, Vol. IV, Parts I and II, 1927), Part I: Pl. 29, No. 2; Pl. 52, No. 14; Pl. 72, No. 5; Pl. 73, No. 10; and Figs. 57, 81, and 84.

[13]J. Alden Mason, "Eskimo Pictorial Art," *The Museum Journal,* XVIII, No. 3 (1927), 252.

[14]Erik Holtved, "Archaeological Investigations in the Thule District," *Meddelelser om Grønland,* CXLI, Part II (1944), 161.

[15]Therkel Mathiassen, *Report on the Expedition* (Report of the Fifth Thule Expedition, Vol. I, Part I, 1945), p. 3.

[16]Henry B. Collins, Jr., "Outline of Eskimo Prehistory," in *Essays in Historical Anthropology of North America* (Smithsonian Miscellaneous Collections, Vol. C, 1940), p. 562. Holtved, "Archaeological Investigations in the Thule District," disagrees with the theory that the Thule culture developed first in Alaska somewhat later than the Old Bering Sea, moved eastward to Canada and Greenland, and, much later, moved back again to Alaska.

of incised ornamentation on utilitarian implements, putting only the scantiest of decoration on harpoon heads.

Thule art gives the impression that the artist did not have time to conceive and execute anything decorative, or that he was leaving the ivory plain merely to enjoy its white expanse. In any event, it is obvious that he had rejected geometric and decorative art for a more representational approach. Gone were fancifully decorated implements and imaginative objects for ceremonial use, and in their place were carved bears, wolves, and ducks, and engraved life sketches.

There is little doubt that these people were the direct forefathers of the nineteenth-century Bering Strait Eskimos who engraved multitudes of scenes on walrus tusks and who sculptured the head of a wolf or bear with the same precision that the Old Bering Sea artist had exercised in his curvilinear designs. They continued at this time to make many dolls and animal figures but began to decorate everyday utensils again. In the Bering Strait region this often took the form of bas-relief animal figures and of simple geometric designs such as the Y, the straight line, and the nucleated circle, while in the southwest Eskimo area the many motifs reminiscent of Ipiutak, Punuk, and Thule began to appear.

The southwest Eskimo area of art in historical times was centered in a triangular area from Nunivak Island to the mouths of the Kuskokwim and Yukon rivers. In several localities this sculptured ivory took on a grotesque aspect with dismembered arms and legs in relief elsewhere on the animal (Figs. 41-43). Sometimes a circle appeared to indicate a joint. These people made bird heads amazingly similar to those of the Scythians who lived in Asia during the fourth century B.C. They covered animals with designs in many colors, not related to the animals themselves but merely as a vehicle for design, and used as many dots and lines as possible on everyday ivory implements. Personal ornaments became popular, and earrings and pendants were created by the hundreds.

The Eskimos of this area, particularly those of Nunivak Island, developed a unique mask utilizing the same ideas of unarticulated limbs and unrelated appurtenances (Figs. 85-88). For example, a mask might have three wooden rings placed around it and numerous carved wooden fish, seals, flippers, or hands with holes in the palms. The rings were a symbolic representation of heaven, earth, and man, and the figurines were the shaman's spiritual helpers. The holed palm was often included so that the season's game would not be held back by the leading spirit, but would flow unobstructed to the hunters.

In the north, while the southwest Eskimo was concentrating on decorating his ivory with geometric designs and painting on wooden objects, the artists were producing the realistic black engravings on white ivory illustrated in such profusion by Hoffman[17] (Figs. 44-52). His publication stemmed from the spirit of the times, one of collecting and preserving the ideas and handiwork of little-known and exotic tribes throughout the world. The book contains invaluable photographs, but should be read critically because, although Hoffman recognizes differences in Alaskan Eskimo art styles, he is reluctant to admit it. Therefore, photographs and discussions alike treat Eskimo art as homogeneous throughout Alaska, disregarding differences that are of fundamental importance.

The graphic ivory art in the nineteenth century, apart from the geometric motifs that already have been noted, was confined to territory north of St. Michael. A great number of tusks and slabs of ivory covered with realistic scenes have been collected from this village, which seemed to be on an artistic boundary line between the north and the south. South of this, to be sure, artists created human and animal figures, but they were semirealistic, often mythical, and were painted on wooden utensils for ceremonial purposes (Fig. 43).

The graphic two-dimensional northern art of this period can be divided into two groups: (1) the so-called hunting tallies, or rows of animals engraved on ivory; and (2) activity representation (Fig. 44). Game tallies supposedly represented a hunter's take of a particular animal during a year or even over a span of years. Consequently, slabs of ivory were often covered with nothing but rows of walrus, caribou, or whale. This was undoubtedly the case for some hunters, but an investigation of the museum collections reveals that repetitious animals were used more often on bag handles and drill bows than on true tallies. This is not to deny the possible use of drill bows and bag handles as hunting scores, but, because the majority of those in the collections are completely filled with figures and are often symmetrical in design, it is evident that the Eskimo artist often used the animal rows for purely esthetic reasons.

[17]Hoffman, *The Graphic Art of the Eskimos*, pp. 739-968.

Of course, there is always the possibility that the hunter might have added a few extra animals just to fill up the spaces.

In the second category there was little that the Eskimo artist did not record. He engraved walrus, whale, seal, and caribou hunts; fishing scenes; village scenes; festivals; and dancing on drill bows, arrow shaft straighteners, bag handles, and pipes. It is not difficult to distinguish the work of one region from another on the basis of the few well-authenticated pieces for each region when examining museum specimens.

The earlier engraved pieces are usually plain slabs of ivory or bone with isolated figures, closely related to the even earlier pictographs found by Mathiassen and Rasmussen. The later ones are whole tusks or bow drills and bag handles engraved with richly detailed scenes of typical activities. These probably were made contemporaneously with the well-known large four- or six-sided pipes, but since many of the latter show whaling ships, a rarity on bow drills, they may have been made later. The majority of the pipes were made on the southern boundary of the northern Bering Strait area, especially around St. Michael. Hoffman states that he was told that they were made at the suggestion of a trader,[18] and there is every reason to believe that this is so since Eskimos had never used flaring pipes. None of the single-figured pictographs and very few of the bow drills and bag handles with scenes come from the region south of the village of St. Michael, so it is probable that the southwest Eskimo did not engrave activity scenes until these had become popular in the north.

So far none of the many-scened bag handles or bow drills has been excavated or attributed to prehistoric peoples. It has even been surmised that the graphic art began only after the Eskimos had come into contact with Europeans. This supposition arose from the fact that early explorers of Alaska could not imagine a "primitive" tribe expressing themselves in such a forceful way without having borrowed the ideas from American or European culture. But, although the first permanent non-Eskimo settlement was established by the Russians in 1784 at Three Saints Bay, Kodiak Island, nothing remotely resembling the northern graphic art has ever come from this vicinity. Furthermore, it is highly improbable that the northern artists had been influenced by the Russians even after

[18]*Ibid.*, p. 854.

the founding of St. Michael for the first sketches were already in existence before the advent of Europeans as revealed at Naujan (Repulse Bay, Canada) and at Cape Prince of Wales (Alaska).

It is also improbable that this early graphic art was influenced by whaling men in the Pacific Ocean since the first whaling ship did not enter the Bering Strait until 1848 and did not go as far north as Point Barrow until 1854. It would have been the Yankee whalers, if any, who were an influence, for they among all sailing people had developed and expanded the distinctive art called scrimshaw.[19] We have proof that the contemporary art was influenced and in part grew out of direct contact with scrimshaw, but it took quite a different course from the earlier nineteenth-century graphic art, which without doubt had had no such contact.

Descriptions by the explorer, Beechey, who sailed to Alaska in 1826, are enough to discount any claim that the northern Eskimos were influenced by whaling art before the latter part of the century. Beechey says about the engraved pieces:

> On the outside of . . . instruments there were etched a variety of figures of men, beasts, and birds, &c. with a truth and character which showed the art to be common among them. The reindeer were generally in herds: in one picture they were pursued by a man in a stooping posture in snowshoes; in another he had approached nearer to his game, and was in the act of drawing his bow. A third represented the manner of taking seals with an inflated skin of the same animal as a decoy; it was placed upon the ice, and not far from it was a man lying upon his belly with a harpoon ready to strike the animal when it should make its appearance. Another was dragging a seal home upon a small sledge; and several baidars were employed harpooning whales which had been previously shot with arrows; and thus by comparing one with another a little history was obtained which gave us a better insight into their habits than could be elicited from any signs or intimations.[20]

When Beechey arrived, the Eskimos already possessed metal and tobacco obtained from Asia through the Little Diomede Island people.

[19]Clifford W. Ashley, *The Yankee Whaler* (New York: Houghton Mifflin Co., 1926), chap. xi.

[20]F. W. Beechey, *Narrative of a Voyage to the Pacific and Beering's Strait, 1825-1828* (London, 1831), Part I, p. 251.

THREE: The Modern Carvers

W HEN the carvers of today say that the "first carving known" was made by Happy Jack and that "there were no carvers when we were young boys," this does not mean that they are ignorant of archeological art. The contemporary artists do not interpret the countless old objects now lodged in museums as having been made by "carvers."

"In the old days," they say, "they made things for their own use," but today they "carve" items for an outside market. The word "carving" has acquired a specific meaning that refers to a certain kind of ivory product outside the sphere of the utilitarian, or even the ceremonial, needs of Eskimos. "Ivory carving" and "carvers of ivory" emerged gropingly after the whalers began plying the northern waters and were fully developed at the turn of the century.

The carvers are aware of the old Eskimo treasures underground, but they consider all of them as belonging to some vague "prehistoric" period. Anything beyond their recollection, whether immediate or handed down, is "thousands of years old," a term that puts the blue Russian trade beads of the nineteenth century and an Okvik harpoon foreshaft of 10 B.C. on equal terms. Some of the carvers keep Okvik harpoon heads, Punuk wrist guards (about sixteenth century A.D.), and nineteenth-century engraved bow drills hidden in their toolboxes, but there is no bridge between the present carving and that of the past. They will say, however, "They did it in the old days, too," when referring to an object dug up from the ground.

They feel no kinship with the long-forgotten artists of the pieces that they treasure. They are not moved by the fact that two thousand years ago an ancestor created an object of esthetic delight as imaginatively and as skillfully as they. In evaluating the span of ivory-carving talent, the art historian is struck by its amazing tenacity for so many hundreds of years. The periods of art—each usually concomitant with a slightly different way of Eskimo life—came and went, but throughout it all was maintained an excellence hard to believe.

Although the contemporary art, with its new styles and viewpoints, seemed to begin abruptly, it nevertheless is just another chapter in the long story of Alaskan Eskimo carving. Thus we speak of the "rich heritage" of the present-day carver, and of his "background of artistic triumphs." The carver himself, however, is the first to become realistic and to explain that the reason he carves so well is because his father began teaching him when he was very, very young. And if a man carved a pleasing object two thousand years ago, that was because his father had taught him, too. Thus, to the carver of today, Eskimo history is not a series of brilliant triumphs but a continuum of fathers teaching their sons to make beautiful things of ivory. So distinctly is parental teaching a part of the carving pattern that in spite of the new attitudes and foreign appurtenances of today, it has been said of a Cape Prince of Wales man who cannot carve: "He did not have a father."

The carving of ivory is man's work. If a woman wanted to carve no one would stop her, but public opinion still keeps her at her furs and away from the traditional carving of men. Furthermore, men have more opportunity to carve since they often learn in a *kazgi* where women are permitted only at certain times. It is where the *kazgis* have weakened, as on St. Lawrence Island and in Nome, that women are beginning to make things of ivory. None of the women on Diomede and King islands carves although several from Diomede occasionally help their husbands polish bracelet links and beads. Sometimes a woman will try her hand at an object to "show" a man that she can do it. On St. Lawrence Island several women are now making plain bracelets and even figurines. The men say that they are good at it and concede that one woman can carve better than her husband.

Not only is carving man's work, but it is something that every man of King and Diomede islands does. The majority of the carvers are real artists, creating lovely figurines and engraving ivory with imagination and talent. Almost the entire adult population, then, is made up of artists, in contrast to those cultures in which the role of artist is highly specialized as it was among the Kwakiutl of the Northwest Coast or, for that matter, in contemporary Europe and America. In the Eskimo culture carving was as important as hunting, and today the two are reciprocal. Without walrus tusks there would be no ivory carving, and without ivory carving there could be no purchase of guns, ammunition, and the other imported gear the Eskimos now use. Hunting is still so important on these islands that not to be a hunter is almost synonymous with poverty. A carver said once, "He is poor; he doesn't go hunting, and so he doesn't have clothes like we have—only white people's clothes."

Nowadays the term, "every man an artist," cannot be applied to the Eskimos of St. Lawrence Island or Nome. Every man of St. Lawrence Island can carve, but some have recently abandoned this activity for more lucrative jobs. In Nome fewer Eskimo men in proportion to the total adult population are engaged in carving, even as part-time work, than on the islands. A number of Eskimo men living in Nome attended school outside of Alaska, returning to take their places in the community but not interested in the traditional Eskimo subsistence pursuits. On rocky Little Diomede and King islands there are no alternatives for the 120 or so persons on each island. They live as closely to the typical Eskimo way of life as is possible today, and, except for a limited amount of seasonal summer work, carving is the only occupation that supplies money.

It is no wonder that every man can carve when the fathers take as active and persuasive a part as they do in the teaching of their children. Even a boy who might leave one of the islands in late boyhood for school elsewhere would already possess the fundamentals of carving learned from his father and other elders. On King Island, in particular, no boy grows up without being surrounded by the talk and actions of carving when men gather in the *kazgi* during the winter between hunting excursions. This is also true of Diomede Island but, because the *kazgis* there are now being used as homes, the carving is more or less carried on in separate households.

The Eskimo carvers believe that a boy cannot become proficient unless he begins very young, practices the same things over and over for years, and handles countless pieces of ivory. A young boy is not supposed to be adept during his first years of carving and will sometimes file for hours without revealing a clue as to what he intends to make. But the youngsters, often only four years old, learn early the feel of tools and ivory in their hands. When the boys are small they are allowed the run of their father's or grandfather's toolbox as long as they do not use the sharpest or most precious tools (Fig. 94). Without permission, but in the presence of a relative, they can rummage in the box for files, sandpaper, and certain gravers.

They usually begin their "carving" by polishing a walrus tooth or shaping a seal, the easiest animal to make. When boys have the opportunities a *kazgi* offers, as on King Island or in King Island Village, they get help from all of the older carvers if they need it. Their progress is checked constantly. For instance, Pikongonna, one of the best King Island carvers, said of his sixteen-year-old boy, "He is not so good yet. I have to get him better in some things."

Another man said, "I let my boy start on a little seal, or a walrus head, and checked him all the time—where to take off a piece here, and how to do it."

Many King Island boys wander into the *kazgi* at King Island Village for a few minutes or hours of carving. They cluster around the display table to check whether or not their fledgling pieces have been sold and to look at the new pieces of the older carvers (Fig. 6).

In spite of the fact that a number of Nome boys had no carving instruction from their fathers they had an opportunity to learn in the old native school, which was consolidated several years ago with the public school. The school board, under the Bureau of Indian Affairs, suggested in the early 1930's that they add ivory carving for the boys and skin sewing for the girls to the curriculum as a potential source of income. Mr. Norman Lee, an excellent carver, and Mrs. Mabel Ramsey, a skilled seamstress, were hired and successfully carried out the program for a number of years. It is doubtful whether a program of this nature could be revived because all children now attend the Nome public school where Eskimo activities are de-emphasized.

The King Island school also presented a course in ivory carving although this island already represented the pinnacle of ivory carving in the Bering Strait. Peter Mayac, another excellent carver, was a hard taskmaster from the reports of those who came under his tutelage, but he got the results that he wanted.

Although it is true that ivory carving is almost completely identified with the Eskimos, this statement requires a certain amount of clarification. The native population of Nome, and that of all the Bering Strait area for that matter, is divided by popular usage into "Eskimos," the full-blooded Eskimos, and "half-breeds," the mixed bloods. Since actual physical heritage is often difficult to ascertain, a number of "Eskimos" are actually mixed bloods who consciously cling to traditional pursuits and values. The people of King and Diomede islands are known as Eskimos, and it is to the Eskimos that the ivory-carving industry belongs. In Nome not every Eskimo is a carver, but almost every carver is an Eskimo.

The work that emerges from the carvers' tools is almost always anonymous, just as it was two thousand years ago and as it has been with almost all primitive art and European craft work. Occasionally a carver will sign his name on an engraved piece, usually a young carver whose work is outstanding and who is eager for approbation outside his own Eskimo group, but this is highly irregular. As a rule one carver can recognize another's carving, in spite of the fact that there is no signature, although to the untrained eye all the carvings look alike.

Several of the exceptionally talented young ivory carvers, spurred by the success of their signed pieces, have forsaken their own cultural milieu for Seattle, where they make designs and patterns for machine-finished bracelets, pendants, and tableware. With their Eskimo hands creating the original design, these items made of elephant, sperm whale, and walrus ivory can without deceit be sold as "Eskimo made." The system is reminiscent of the medieval guild crafts, with a master artist creating the original design and artisans completing the remainder of the work. In this case, however, the piece is always signed, and the artist receives the recognition to which the medieval man was not accustomed.

At the present writing there are also several Eskimo men who call themselves "Eskimo artists" but never have been ivory carvers. Two of the most publicized are George Ahgupuk and Robert Mayokok. Ahgupuk has created a unique medium from bleached reindeer skin. His most typical and, indeed, extremely striking works were used as illustrations in a collection of Eskimo legends.[1] Mayokok has written several small booklets about Eskimo life, illustrating them with pen-and-ink drawings. He also sells line drawings for framing.

These two men were not, however, the first Eskimos to use media other than ivory for line drawings. In 1903, for example, a trader interested a young southwest Alaskan Eskimo named Guy Kakarook in making crayon sketches of the world around him (Fig. 58). His initial attempts were extraordinarily competent and are now in the United States National Museum.

[1]Edward L. Keithahn, *Igloo Tales* (Education Division, U.S. Indian Service; Lawrence, Kans.: Haskell Institute, 1945).

FOUR: Ivory, Tough and Temperamental

No ESKIMO can carve without ivory, and, although the Bering Strait artist lives in the world's richest walrus grounds, the ivory is sometimes hard to come by. The walrus is a fairly predictable creature as he makes his twice-yearly migration through the Bering Strait, but, when his migratory mechanism tells him to travel nearer to the Russian side of the strait, the American Eskimos are out of luck. Fortunately, King and Little Diomede islands are usually in the center of the migration and can count on a good hunting season.

Walrus hunting is probably the most important single activity of these islands. Oomiaks with their eight- or nine-man crews go out as long as the walrus are in sight because without the walrus there would be no food and, most important of all today, no ivory.

The present importance of ivory has led to changes in the division of the spoils after walrus hunts. Only thirty years ago the division was still according to the tradition described by Curtis: "In dividing a walrus, the boat-owner [of King Island] receives the flippers, and half each of the blubber, heart, liver and intestines; the harpooner takes the ivory; the remainder is divided equally amongst the crew."[1]

Ivory at that time was more plentiful, not because the walrus were more numerous but because the Eskimos gathered tons of "fossil" ivory from the shores of Siberia as well as from archeological sites on the American side. They are now cut off from their Siberian supply and

[1]Edward S. Curtis, *The North American Indian* (Norwood, Mass., 1930), XX, 101.

have emptied their own reservoirs so that they are almost wholly dependent on newly caught ivory. They look back with longing on memories of their fathers' selling gunny sacks full of polished ivory tusks for only a few dollars. "If we only had some of that now, what we wouldn't do with it!" they exclaim.

The division of ivory has been revised nowadays so that each man receives an almost equal share. The meat is divided after each hunt as in the past, but the tusks are kept until the end of the season and then apportioned equally among the men who made up the crew that year, the captain (boat owner) and the harpooner getting first choice. The number of tusks varies from year to year depending on the catch. In 1955, for instance, Pikongonna received twenty tusks as his share, but only one tusk during the previous season when hunting was poor. The ivory is divided in this manner on Diomede Island, also, but Nome hunters usually divide it after each excursion because they do not go hunting as often as the islanders.

Although the only sure way of getting ivory is to participate in a walrus hunt, there are other ways. For example, sometimes a carver who has a surplus of ivory will "loan" a tusk to another, expecting to be repaid at a later date, preferably when he, himself, is running low on ivory.

Sometimes a carver buys ivory from the cooperative store on his island or from one of the commercial stores in Nome. Occasionally a carver will sell or trade his raw ivory to the cooperative store if he needs cash or food immediately, possibly buying it back at a higher price at a later date. The carvers often refuse to buy ivory from the Nome stores, however, because of the high price, although without it they may be unable to carve for a time. Some will never buy it as a matter of principle because they know that the trader has bought it very cheaply when the carvers needed a few "quick" dollars, and that in order to regain it they would have to pay from two to four times the selling price.

The King Island carvers always appear to have more raw ivory than the Diomede Islanders although the latter are excellent and fearless hunters. The Diomeders sell raw ivory to dealers when they need money more often than the King Islanders, and this makes the latter very indignant. When Diomede carvers wanted to buy ivory from them one summer, one said, "We have lots of ivory and they have hardly any.

But the summer before, they had lots of raw ivory and we didn't have enough to carve, and they went and sold lots of it to a store. It almost made me sick. And now this year they haven't got ivory. They could have used that ivory this year to carve instead of selling it as raw ivory last year."

Sometimes ivory is traded for a service rendered. This practice is comparatively rare and sometimes is only a device whereby ivory can be given to a well-liked carver who needs it but is too proud to ask. A Nome carver, old and unable to hunt, made snowshoes in 1955 for a man who wanted to give him a large tusk.

Although walrus ivory is looked upon as the primary carving medium, every scrap of material that can be called ivory is utilized. This includes mammoth and mastodon tusks, the teeth of the sperm whale, walrus, and even seal. In a pinch elephant ivory might be used.

Of these sources the mammoth, a species of elephant whose gigantic tusks have lain for thirty thousand years in the frozen arctic soil, is the most important. It is not so popular as walrus ivory because of its limitations in spite of the large tusks. Fresh mammoth ivory undoubtedly was indistinguishable from elephant ivory, which is cross-hatched in appearance and solid in form. But, with the passing of millennia, the laminated layers of which the tusk is composed have loosened, revealing in cross section a set of closely fitted gray or brown ivory rings. Because each ring is rarely more than an inch or two thick, the carvers can make only small animals, thin paper knives, and bracelets. The condition of the ivory, moreover, is often not good enough for even that. Sometimes the ivory is "just like clay," and then it is good for nothing. Mastodon ivory is very similar to mammoth, but very scarce.

A popular ivory, but very costly because of its route from tropical waters via the Alaskan trader, is sperm whale tooth. The Eskimos became acquainted with this kind of ivory from the whalers who either engraved a tooth with fashionable damsels from *Godey's Lady's Book* or with dramatic representations of the American flag and the eagle or made unadorned cribbage boards from it. Each of the fifty or so teeth of the sperm whale's gigantic lower jaw is a fairly homogenous piece of ivory, not crosshatched like elephant ivory, and not with a mottled core like a walrus tusk. This homogeneity is occasionally very desirable in small figurines, rings, and small cribbage boards, but because the price for an uncarved two-pound tooth is from five to ten dollars, the carver will use it only for special orders when he is assured of a good price. The carvers also like this kind of ivory because of its toughness and resistance to splintering.

They use the tooth of the walrus but are restricted by its small size to the making of pendants, watch fobs, bracelet links, and minute animals. The patterns of the dentine and the outer part of the tooth are often quite striking when they are discolored.

The Eskimos rarely carve imported elephant ivory because the traders in Alaska urge carvers to use only native materials. In spite of the fact that sperm whale ivory is not an indigenous material, it has been identified with contemporary carving ever since the whalers brought it with them, and it is as much a part of the carving industry today as are the imported lead pencil and India ink used to blacken incised lines.

The terminology associated with ivory carving is often arbitrary and misleading. Carvers and noncarvers alike use a number of ambiguous terms. The term "carving" seems somewhat incongruous when one watches an Eskimo carver shape an ivory bear with a hacksaw, file, graver, and sandpaper. Nevertheless, all ivory work is known as "ivory carving" to everybody, and all persons who work with ivory are "carvers" no matter what tool they use.

The term "carving" is used also in another and more limited sense to refer only to figurines and the more intricately shaped vases, paper knives, and so forth. Two-dimensional work of blackened, incised figures and scenes or geometric designs is called "etching" or "etched work." No one uses the term "sculpture" even for the best figurines, but "engraving" is occasionally used alternatively with "etching."

In this book, "carving" denotes the shaping of raw ivory into any object, whether figurine, harpoon head, or paper knife, but "sculpture" refers only to figurines. "Engraving" is used when speaking of incised lines either in a realistic composition or in an abstract design.

The Bering Strait carver considers walrus ivory a temperamental material and spends a lifetime learning its characteristics. He divides walrus ivory into "green," "new," and "old" ivory. Green ivory is white ivory that has been extracted from the walrus but not yet seasoned by drying. New ivory is white, seasoned ivory, and old ivory is any color other than white, ranging from light cream to orange, purple, or black.

The mere fact that ivory is colored means that it is old, for it takes a number of years to discolor. But, although a new, white piece of ivory will turn a creamish color after a few years' contact with the air, the term "old ivory" usually is restricted to the multicolored tusks that have lain for decades or even centuries in mineral and vegetable matter. The most colorful of all have been buried in salt-water beaches. The wide range of colors found in old walrus ivory is not found in the mammoth, which is usually either gray, light tan, or brown. Old ivory has mistakenly been called "fossil ivory," a misleading term because it implies that the ivory has become a different substance through displacement of secondary materials. The only change, however, has been in color.

The present-day carvers closely guard their pieces of old ivory because the most fruitful sources of it are the beaches on the Siberian side of the Bering Strait. King Island carvers who made a trip to Siberia a decade ago still make bracelets, one at a time, from their diminishing supply. "The Russians have all the old ivory now," the Eskimos in Nome complain, but those of St. Lawrence Island still gather tusks washed out of their beaches, which are very close to Siberia. The gathering of old ivory is regulated there by the village councils of Savoonga and Gambell, and it is usually sold through official channels either to St. Lawrence Island Eskimos or to the Bureau of Indian Affairs. An Eskimo from King or Diomede Island rarely gets one of these tusks.

For a number of years, despite the Federal Antiquity Act (1906), many Eskimos looted old village sites on government-owned land for large ivory tools. After the establishment of Marks Field, an air base, in 1941, publicity was given to the act to forestall wholesale robbery of the sites near Nome. Although these tools are not as colorful as ivory from salt-water beaches, the usual brown discolorations qualify them as "old" ivory. Bracelets and other jewelry made from it cost from two to four times as much as new ivory.

Occasionally over the years a few carvers, usually abetted by a trader, have tried to color ivory artificially. They have experimented with every substance within their knowledge, but the most popular and successful were tea, coffee, ink, tar, and crude oil. Boiled for hours and even days in these materials, the ivory emerged tan or dark brown, and this to the casual purchaser of ivory meant "old" ivory. The carvers also attempted to color with crepe paper, a material commonly used for dyeing bleached skins, but without success. The frauds were detected eventually, and, because feeling ran so high about the deception, the carvers rarely color ivory now. However, an occasional wholesaler in the United States continues to color brooches, pendants, earrings, and cuff links artificially.

The uniqueness of old walrus ivory lies in the number of colors found in one tusk and the designs they make in the cellular composition of the tusk. Even tan or brown old ivory usually has striations of deeper color forming a delicate radiating pattern when viewed in cross section. Although the ivory will turn numerous colors, none is very pale or very brilliant; the deeper, more somber, hues predominate. For this reason, the promoters of artificial coloring did not attempt to dye their ivory in the manner of the ivory carvers of India.[2] These carvers colored their ivory, not in order to deceive, but for specific decorative effects resulting from the contrast to the natural whiteness of the ivory. The Hawaiians, too, color their ivory ornaments "by wrapping in ki leaves and exposing to the smoke of burning sugar cane."[3]

Probably one of the cleverest deceptions was the simulation of jade several hundred years ago in Peking. The mottled core of the walrus ivory was stained with verdigris, and this later became a standard decorative treatment of walrus ivory.[4]

The bleaching of discolored ivory, as in the restoration of many old, yellowed, elephant ivory carvings of medieval times, has never been tried.

Walrus ivory is further classified as "carved" or "raw," the latter being merely uncarved green, new, or old ivory.

The two most common complaints in the carving of walrus ivory are its propensity to split and the presence of the mottled core in each tusk.

[2]"Ivory may be dyed in various colours. The crimson red colour commonly seen is given by dipping the ivory for a short time into a mordant of nitromuriate of tin, and then plunging it into a bath of Brazil wood, cochineal, or a mixture of those substances. A scarlet tint is produced by lac dye, and if the scarlet ivory be plunged into a solution of potash, it changes to cherry red. A yellow dye may be produced by giving the ivory the tin mordant and digesting it at a gentle heat in a clear decoction of fustic. A black dye may be given by boiling the ivory in a strained decoction of logwood, and then steeping it in a solution of red sulphate, or red acetate of iron" (Cecil K. Burns, "A Monograph on Ivory Carving," *The Journal of Indian Art and Industry,* IX, No. 75 [1901], 54).

[3]Bishop Museum, *Hawaiian Collections,* Handbook, Part I, 1915, p. 53.

[4]Schuyler Cammann, "Carvings in Walrus Ivory," *University Museum Bulletin,* XVIII, No. 3 (1954), 21-22.

[TEXT CONTINUES ON PAGE 94]

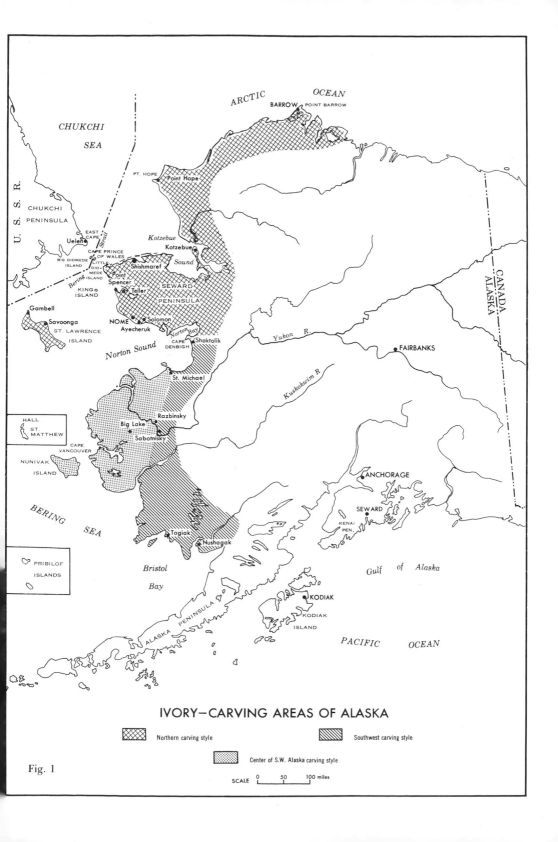

IVORY–CARVING AREAS OF ALASKA

Northern carving style   Southwest carving style

Center of S.W. Alaska carving style

SCALE 0   50   100 miles

Fig. 1

Fig. 2. Nome at the time of the gold rush, July, 1900

Fig. 3. Nome from the air, 1948. Photograph by William A. Shepherd

Fig. 4. King Island Village, a mile east of Nome

Fig. 5. The *kazgi* at King Island Village where the carvers work. The open door faces the Bering Sea

Fig. 6. A young carver places his carvings on the display table. The carvers are working in the background

Fig. 7. Happy Jack and his family, 1908. Photograph by H. G. Kaiser, from the collection of
Catherine Bongard and Irene Bongard Shearer

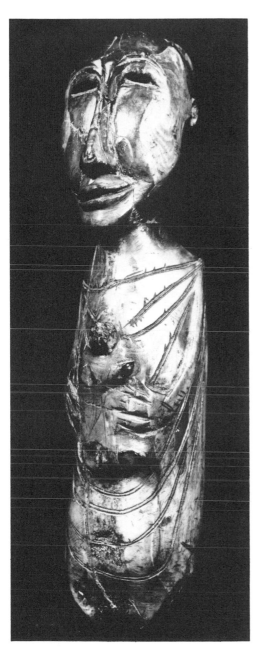 

Fig. 8. The "Okvik Madonna," found on St. Lawrence Island. Height, 17.2 cm. University of Alaska Museum 4-1934-607

Fig. 9. Another view of the "Okvik Madonna"

Fig. 10. An Okvik figurine from St. Lawrence Island. Height, 17.5 cm. University of Alaska Museum 1-1931-970

Fig. 11. Okvik figurines. The figure on the left is 15 cm. high. University of Alaska Museum

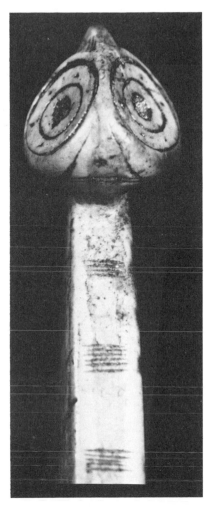

Fig. 12. Figurine, probably Okvik, provenience unknown, collected by A. Hrdlička. Height, 19.2 cm. U. S. National Museum 390551

Fig. 13. Okvik bird head from St. Lawrence Island, a greatly magnified section of an ulu (woman's knife). The head is actually only 1.5 cm. long. University of Alaska Museum

Fig. 14. Okvik object, presumably a lance head, from St. Lawrence Island. Length, about 16.8 cm. University of Alaska Museum

Fig. 15. Okvik harpoon heads. The one on the left is 9.4 cm. long. University of Alaska Museum

Fig. 16. Okvik harpoon heads. The one on the right is about 5.8 cm. long. University of Alaska Museum

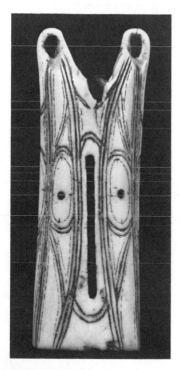

Fig. 17. Unidentified object, presumably Old Bering Sea, from St. Lawrence Island. The same design is engraved on the reverse. Length, 7 cm. University of Alaska Museum 1-27-193

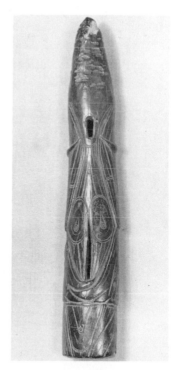

Fig. 18. Object assigned to Old Bering Sea, but with characteristic Okvik motifs, collected by A. Hrdlička. Length, 20 cm. U. S. National Museum 333040

Fig. 19. Old Bering Sea harpoon heads from St. Lawrence Island. The one on the right is 11.6 cm. long. University of Alaska Museum *(left to right)* 1-27-305, no number, "Kukulik 1935"

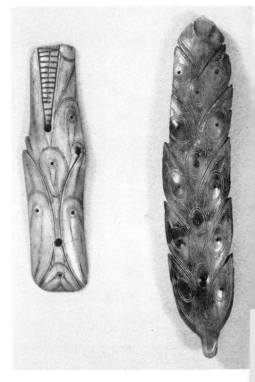

Fig. 20. Old Bering Sea objects from Miyowagahameet, St. Lawrence Island. The one on the right is an unusually beautiful piece. Photograph from the Smithsonian Institution

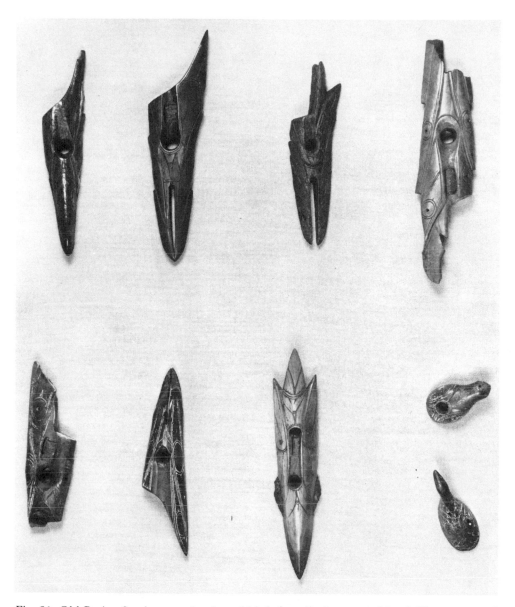

Fig. 21. Old Bering Sea harpoon heads and birds from St. Lawrence Island. The one second from the left, top row, is 9.2 cm. long. University of Alaska Museum *(top, left to right)* M-1977, 1440K, 070, 1-27-305; *(bottom, left to right)* number obliterated, 1-1927-2470, "Kukulik 1935," no numbers

Fig. 22. Old Bering Sea harpoon head, showing the top and two sides. Approximately two-thirds actual size. Drawing by Gerald Fromberg, from a rubbing.

Fig. 23. Unidentified Punuk object, possibly a wrist guard, from St. Lawrence Island. Height, 8.2 cm. University of Alaska Museum 1-1926-877-a

Fig. 24. Unidentified Punuk object. Height, 14.3 cm. University of Alaska Museum M-2576

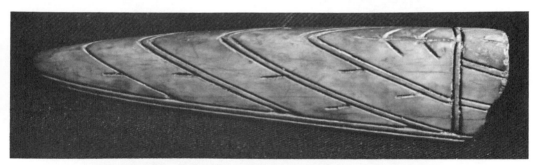

Fig. 25. Unidentified Punuk object from St. Lawrence Island. University of Alaska Museum

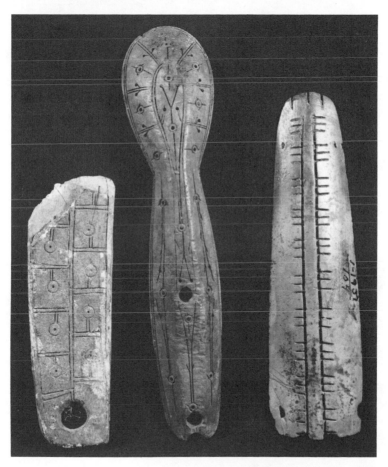

Fig. 26. Typical Punuk objects, use unknown, approximately two-thirds natural size. University of Alaska Museum *(right)* 1-1937-104

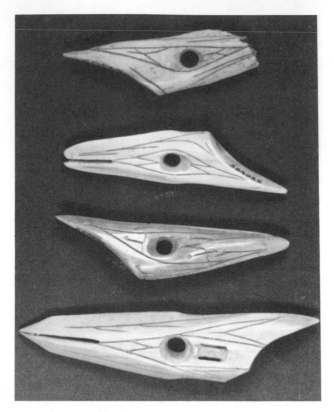

Fig. 27. Early Punuk harpoon heads from St. Lawrence
Island. The one at the bottom is 10.2 cm. long. U. S.
National Museum *(top to bottom)* 343219, 364025, 364025,
343494

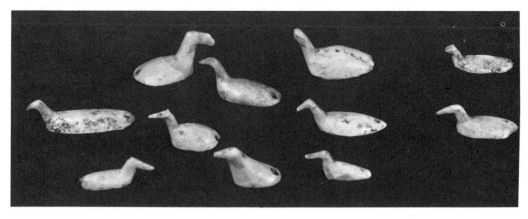

Fig. 28. Thule flat-bottomed birds from St. Lawrence Island, used
in the game of *Tingmiujaq*. The bird on the left is 3.2 cm. long.
U. S. National Museum 346407

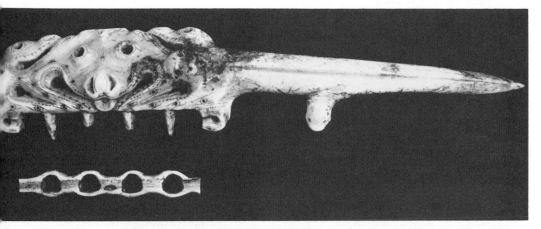

Fig. 29. Unidentified object, probably Ipiutak, from Point Spencer. The principal face is double, with the eyes common to both. The second face is clearly visible at the top of Figure 30. Length, 26.8 cm.
University of Alaska Museum

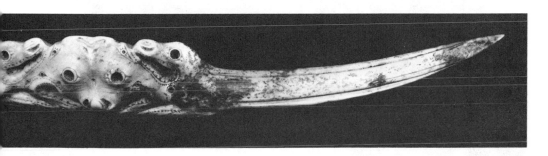

Fig. 30. Another view of Figure 29, showing the double face in the center

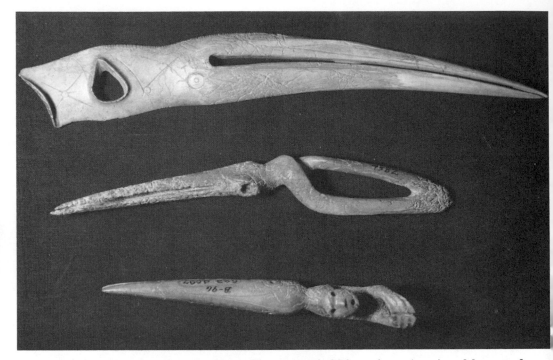

Fig. 31. Ipiutak objects from Pt. Hope. The top one is 26.8 cm. long. American Museum of Natural History *(top to bottom)* 60.2-3970, 60.1-7582, 60.2-4097

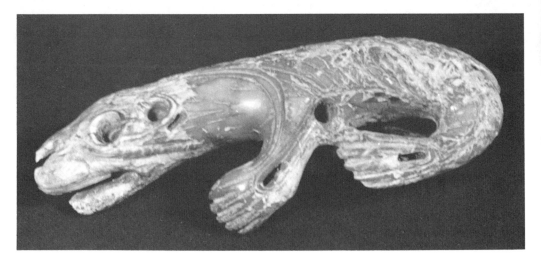

Fig. 32. Ipiutak walrus figurine from Pt. Hope. Length, 10 cm. American Museum of Natural History 60.1-7665

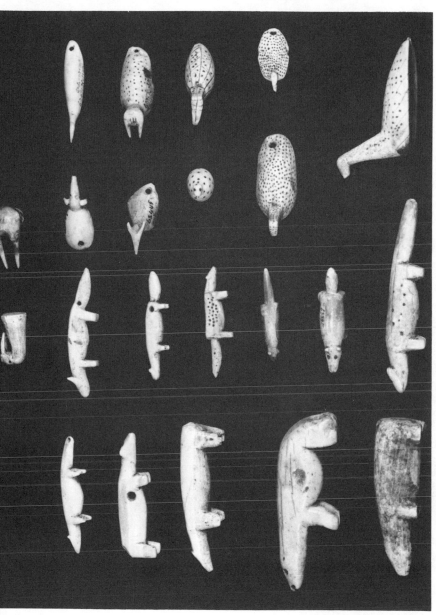

Fig. 33. Animals and birds from St. Lawrence Island, collected by E. W. Nelson. Some of these were undoubtedly excavated by the Eskimos and belong in the prehistoric Thule period. The bear in the lower left corner is 9.3 cm. long. U. S. National Museum (*top row, left to right*) 63400, 63402, 63458, 63471; (*second row, left to right*) 63428, 63479; (*third row, left to right*) 63398, 63401, 63445, 63433; (*fourth row, left to right*) 63396, 63672, 63417, 63464; (*fifth row, left to right*) 63391, 63409, 63452, 63476; (*sixth row, left to right*) 126997, 63395; (*bottom row, left to right*) 63304, 63452

Fig. 34. Ivory human figures from Cape Prince of Wales, collected in 1905. The facial expressions on the two at the bottom, right, are unusual; although catalogued as from Cape Prince of Wales, these are possibly from southwest Alaska. The top, right, figure is 6 cm. high. University Museum, University of Pennsylvania *(top row, left to right)* NA-1109, NA-1109, NA-1109, NA-1110, NA-1111, NA-1113; *(middle row, left to right)* NA-1114, NA-1115, NA-1116, NA-1117, NA-1119, NA-1120; *(bottom row, left to right)* NA-1121, NA-1122, NA-1123, NA-1124, NA-1127, NA-1128

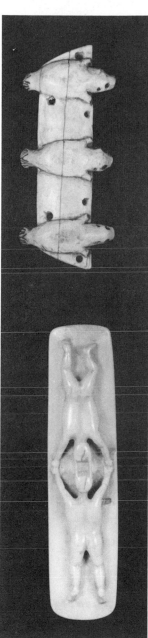
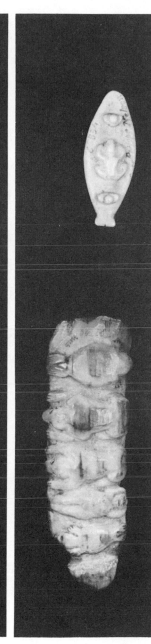
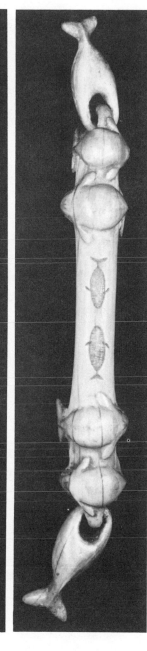

Fig. 35. Nineteenth-century walrus ivory bas-relief carvings from northern Alaska. U. S. National Museum (*top row, left to right*) 360375 ("hair-pulling contest at Nome" collected by V. J. Evans), 44865 (from Sledge Island); (*middle row, left to right*) 37749 (provenience unknown), 63834 (from Pt. Hope); (*bottom*) 44690 (from Sledge Island)

Fig. 36. Unique handle for an ulu (woman's knife) collected at Pt. Hope, 1885. The handle, of walrus ivory, has turned very brown. The eyes are inset first with wood and then with a black bead. Length, 13.5 cm. U. S. National Museum 76680

Fig. 37. Late nineteenth-century wooden figure, removable head, equipped with a thong for hanging. Height, about 22 cm. American Museum of Natural History 60.1-4301

Fig. 38. Another view of Figure 37

Fig. 39. Ivory figurines from Razbinsky and Sabotnisky on the lower Yukon River. The figure at the far left is 20.2 cm. high. Nos. 47070, 48908, 49005, 49007 and 69067 have grooves incised completely around the head behind the face. U. S. National Museum *(far left)* 48709; *(top row, left to right)* 48711, 47070, 48710, 49005; *(far right)* 49006; *(bottom row, left to right)* 48713, 69067, 48907, 48908

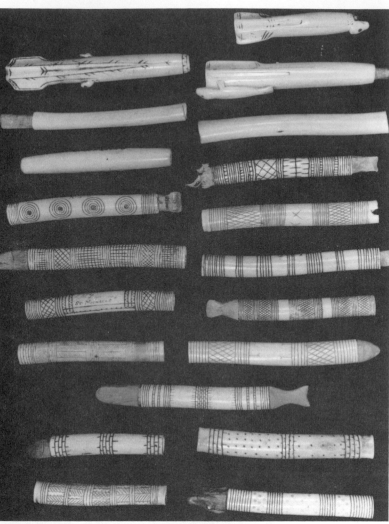

Fig. 41. Needlecases collected about 1880, the six plain ones from the vicinity of Cape Nome, the others from southwest Alaska (Nunivak Island, Big Lake, Razbinsky, and St. Michael). The one in the top row marked "St. Michaels" (No. 129231) is 10.3 cm. long. U. S. National Museum (*top row, left to right*) 24475 (from St. Michael), 48328 (from Nunivak Island), 36736 (with wooden plug on either end; from Big Lake), 48807 (from lower Yukon River), 129231 (from St. Michael), 37802 (from Cape Vancouver), 49028 (from Razbinsky), 45337 (from Cape Nome), 44125 (from Koyuk), 176230 (from Cape Nome; the little animals have inlaid eyes); (*bottom row, left to right*) 36768 (from Big Lake; the wooden head has ivory inlaid eyes), 48604 (from Razbinsky), 38184 (from lower Yukon River), 36781 (provenience unknown), 24492 (from St. Michael), 48803 (from Razbinsky), 36763 (from Big Lake), 44743 (from Sledge Island), 24469 (from Norton Sound), 48800 (provenience unknown, probably from Cape Nome)

Fig. 40. Nineteenth-century dolls from the lower Yukon River. The one on the left is 18.2 cm. high. U. S. National Museum (*left to right*) 48858 (ivory and cloth), 32914 (ivory and sealskin), no number (wood and sealskin)

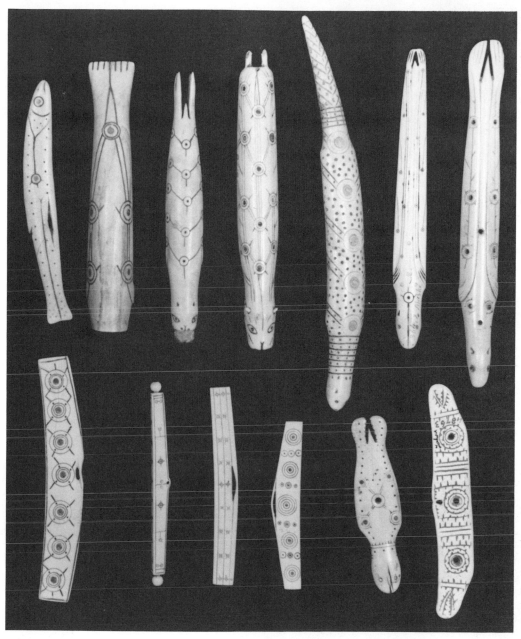

Fig. 42. Bag handles and fasteners collected by E. W. Nelson and Mr. Applegate from south-west Alaska (Togiak and lower Yukon and Kuskokwim rivers). All these have similar decoration on the reverse except No. 48867, which is plain. The one in the top left-hand corner is 10.5 cm. long. U. S. National Museum *(top row, left to right)* 48763, 48869, 127469, 127469, 127469, 127469; *(bottom row, left to right)* 48860, 36479, 48867, 38128, 27443, 43699, 35972

Fig. 43. A typical design from southwest Alaska, taken from the bowl of a wooden spoon from lower Kuskokwim River, late nineteenth century. Length, 13 cm. Collection of D. J. Ray

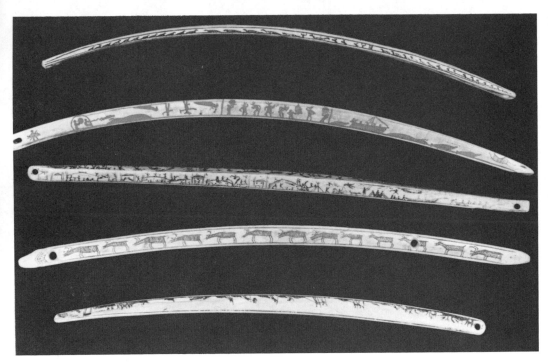

Fig. 44. Engraved drill bows and bag handles, presumably from the early nineteenth century but collected about 1880 in northern Alaska. U.S. National Museum (*top to bottom*) no number, 48522, no number, 24554, no number

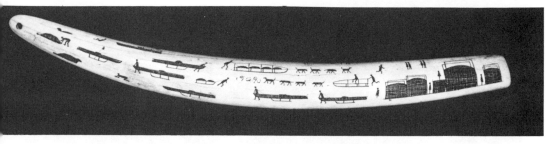

Fig. 45. Engraved tusk collected in 1896, provenience undesignated but presumably from near St. Michael or farther north. U. S. National Museum 19090

Fig. 46. Reverse of Figure 45

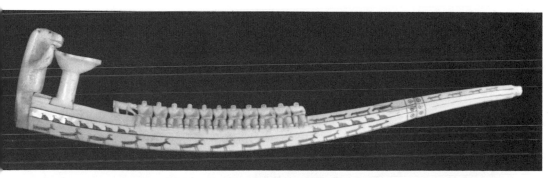

Fig. 47. Ivory pipe, provenience unknown but undoubtedly from northern Alaska. Length, 40.5 cm. University Museum, University of Pennsylvania, NA-9388

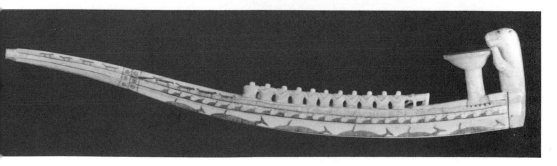

Fig. 48. Reverse of Figure 47

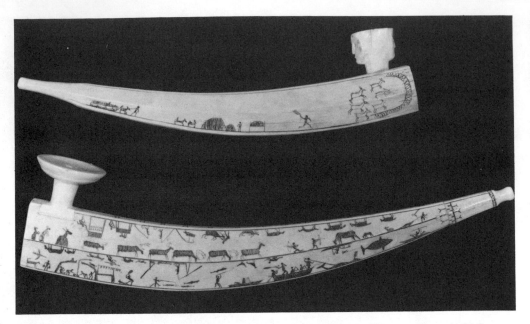

Fig. 49. Two unusual pipes from Port Clarence. Length *(top)*, 27 cm.; *(bottom)*, 35.2 cm.
American Museum of Natural History *(top)* 60-1229; *(bottom)* 19-434

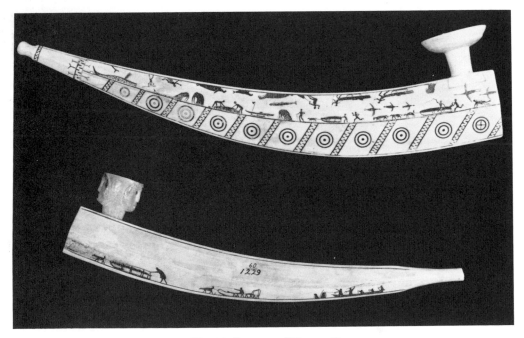

Fig. 50. Reverse of Figure 49

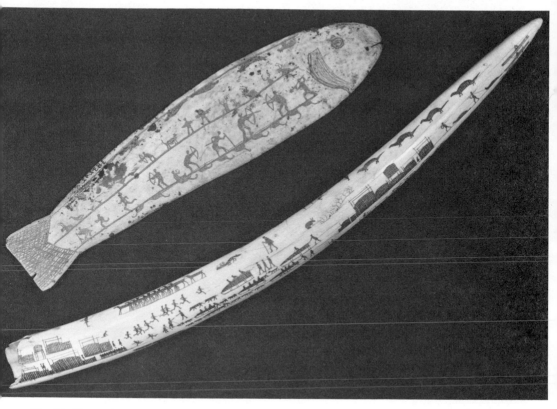

Fig. 51. Engravings on bone and walrus ivory. The one at the top, in the shape of a fish, is of bone. The walrus tusk at the bottom is 44.5 cm. long. U. S. National Museum *(top)* 383242; *(bottom)* 383239

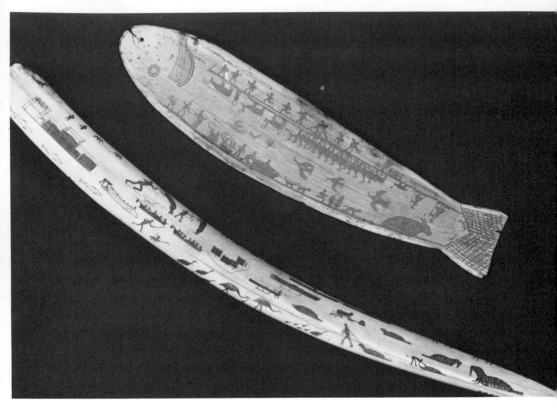

Fig. 52. Reverse of Figure 51

Fig. 53. Facsimile in ivory of a soap wrapper, engraved by Happy Jack on an old mattock. Historical Museum, Mystic Seaport, Conn. Photograph by Verne F. Ray

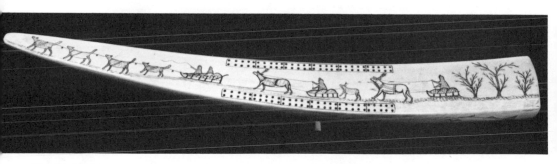

Fig. 54. Walrus tusk cribbage board made in 1903 by Happy Jack. This is one of the first cribbage boards made in Nome, and one of the finest of its kind. Collection of Mr. and Mr. Ralph Hawley, Bothell, Wash. Length, 58.5 cm.

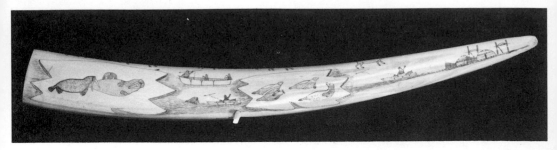

Fig. 55. Reverse of Figure 54. Note the same scene at the tip of the tusk as on the napkin ring in Figure 56

Fig. 56. Magnification of a napkin ring made by Happy Jack in 1903. Actual outside circumference, 17 cm. Collection of Mr. and Mr. Ralph Hawley

Fig. 57. Billiken bank, patented 1908, prototype of ivory billiken. Collection of D. J. Ray

Fig. 58. Crayon sketch by Guy Kakarook, about 1903, of the river steamer *Michael* at a steamboat fueling landing, one of many on the Yukon River at that time. From the collection of the artist's sketches in the U. S. National Museum. Photograph from the Smithsonian Institution

Fig. 59. Wood carving of woman and baby from St. Lawrence Island, carved by Numayuk in the 1920's. Height, 14.4 cm. University of Alaska Museum. See also Figures 60 and 61. These carvings were supposedly given to sterile women

Fig. 60. Wood carvings by Numayuk. See explanation of Figure 59. *(Left)* old man, height 13.8 cm., University of Alaska Museum 1-1927-491; *(right)* old woman, height, 11.2 cm., University of Alaska Museum

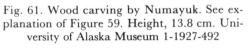

Fig. 61. Wood carving by Numayuk. See explanation of Figure 59. Height, 13.8 cm. University of Alaska Museum 1-1927-492

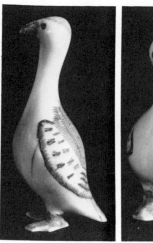

Fig. 63. Two snowbirds—one in summer plumage, the other in winter plumage—carved by Aloysius Pikongonna of King Island. Collection of D. J. Ray

Fig. 62. Eider ducks carved by a St. Lawrence carver about 1947. The shorter one on the right is 4.2 cm. high. The black markings are made with graphite; the feet and bill are colored with hematite. Collection of D.J. Ray

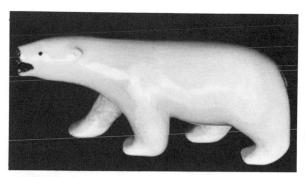

Fig. 64. The finished polar bear shown being carved by Pikongonna in Figures 96-107. Length, 12.5 cm. Collection of D. J. Ray

Fig. 65. Ship of ivory and baleen made by a Diomede Island Eskimo about 1953. Length, about 2 feet. These ships cost around $250 or $300, are rarely made, and are collectors' items.

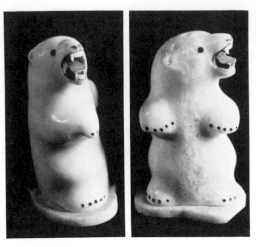

Fig. 66. Contemporary salt and pepper shakers.
Height, 5.5 cm. Collection of D. J. Ray

Fig. 67. Ivory objects made about 1948. The birds are from St.
Lawrence Island; the polar bear was carved by Pikongonna of King
Island; the billiken and rabbit are by local carvers in Nome. Height
of the billiken, 4 cm. Collection of D. J. Ray

Fig. 68. An example of the elaborately carved Nunivak Island tusks. This remarkable tusk
was carved in the 1920's by an unknown carver. Collection of Robert A. Henning, Edmonds,
Wash.

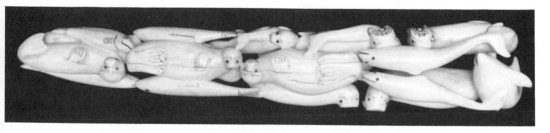

Fig. 69. Another view of Figure 68

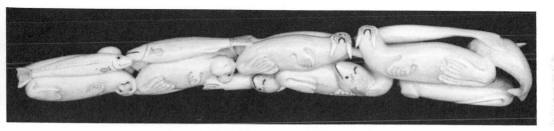

Fig. 70. Another view of Figure 68

Fig. 71. Another view of Figure 68

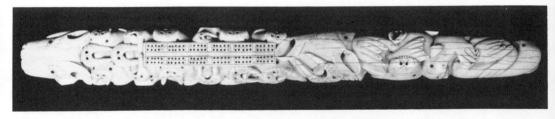

Fig. 72. Cribbage board, another example of the Nunivak Island art of the 1920's. Length, 65 cm. American Museum of Natural History 60.2-5381A

Figure 73. Reverse of Figure 72

Fig. 74. Nunivak tusk, about 1924. The eyes are inset with ivory and baleen; mouths are orange-red; eyebrows and whiskers are black; gills of fish are red; ears of one fox are orange-red. Length, 87 cm. U. S. National Museum 332176

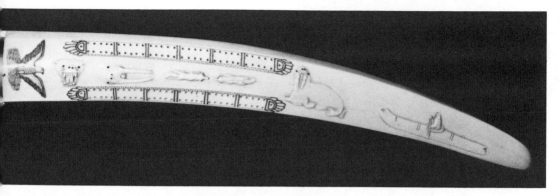

Fig. 75. Cribbage board from northern Alaska, about 1926, illustrating the early use of a bear's head which was once thought to have been suggested by army insignia. Collection of Mrs. Antoinette Hotovitsky, Seattle, Wash.

Fig. 76. Two pendants made by Happy Jack in 1903. The bear pendant is 5.5 cm. wide; the man pendant is 2.9 cm. wide. The filigree beads are not Eskimo made. Collection of Mr. and Mrs. Ralph Hawley

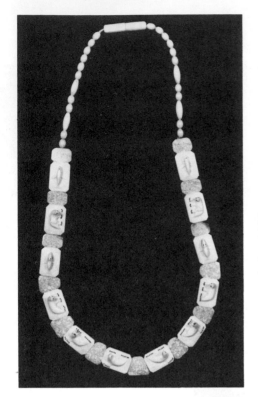

Fig. 77. Necklace of walrus ivory from Little Diomede Island made about 1955. The pieces interspersed between the carved animals are very yellowed walrus ivory core. Length, 55 cm. Collection of D. J. Ray

Fig. 78. Contemporary ivory jewelry. Animal bracelet by carver from Little Diomede Island. Etched bracelet by Shishmaref carver; outside circumference, 20¾ cm. Dog-team bracelet by Ozenna, Sr., of Diomede Island. Necklace made of old ivory in Nome; length, 35 cm. Collection of D. J. Ray

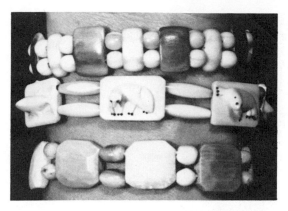

Fig. 79. Contemporary ivory bracelets. The middle animal bracelet, which always has six links of six different animals, was made by a Diomede carver. The two plain bracelets, of tan ivory, are greatly admired by ivory carvers because they are put together with hand-made, rather than machine-turned, beads. Top from Solomon; bottom from Shishmaref. Collection of D. J. Ray

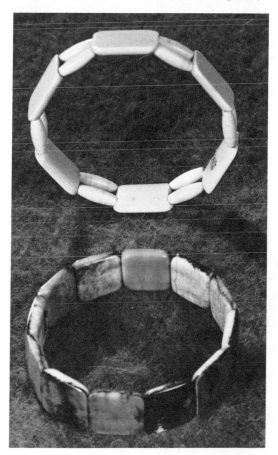

Fig. 80. Plain bracelets of walrus ivory. The top one is of "green" ivory; the bottom one of "old" ivory. Collection of D. J. Ray

Fig. 81. Simple contemporary **walrus** ivory necklaces. The darker colors are browns, tans, and yellows. The one on the left, with squarish beads, was supposedly traded from East Cape, Siberia, about 1948. The longest necklace is 60 cm. Collection of D. J. Ray

Fig. 82. Bear-head bracelet and necklace set by a Diomede Island carver. Baleen is inset in nose and eyes; the markings are made with India ink. Note the whiskers. Each link is about 1¾ cm. long and 1½ cm. wide

Fig. 83. Driftwood masks from King Island, about 1915. These are simple in concept in contrast to those from southwest Alaska. The one on the left, 17.2 cm. high, has red color around the mouth. University Museum, University of Pennsylvania *(left)* NA-4566; *(right)* NA-4572

Fig. 84. Early twentieth-century mask from Unalakleet. Collection of D. J. Ray

Fig. 85. Modern mask, 1950, from Hooper Bay. Height, 32.8 centimeters. University of Alaska UA 492

Fig. 86. Mask from Nunivak Island. The face represents a female seal, characterized by the down-turned mouth, and the circular hoops represent various layers of space. University Museum, University of Pennsylvania, NA-6384. Photograph courtesy of the University Museum

Fig. 87. Mask from Hooper Bay region, possibly late nineteenth or early twentieth century. University Museum, University of Pennsylvania, NA-10348. Photograph courtesy of the University Museum

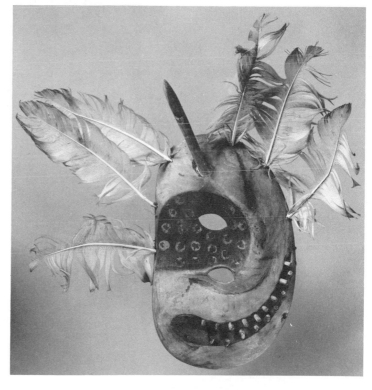

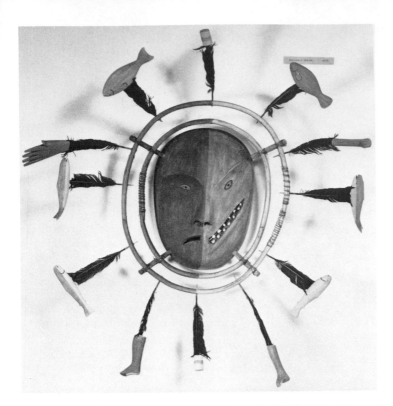

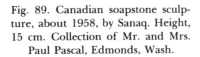

Fig. 88. Mask from Nunivak Island, 1940s. The rings represent heaven and earth; the objects stuck into the rings represent the *angokok's* (shaman's) spiritual helpers. Washington State Museum 4516

Fig. 89. Canadian soapstone sculpture, about 1958, by Sanaq. Height, 15 cm. Collection of Mr. and Mrs. Paul Pascal, Edmonds, Wash.

Fig. 90. Samnarana using an adz on a tusk supported on a driftwood stump. The very old oval driftwood box used for holding his tools is on his left. This photograph, and the others that follow of the carvers at work, was taken at King Island Village *kazgi* under very difficult light conditions and with the carvers unaware that they were being photographed

Fig. 91. Samnarana using a graver on a small cribbage board

Fig. 92. Bob Omiak, of Little Diomede, making a small billiken. Note the use of the foot as a prop; also the file and the hand vise

Fig. 93. An unknown Eskimo using a bow drill in 1919. This would actually never be used on a crib bage board after it was completed, as this one is, but the photograph illustrates how it was used. Bow drills today are exactly like this one, and used in exactly the same manner. Photograph by Henry G Kaiser, from the collection of Catherine Bongard and Irene Bongard Shearer

Fig. 94. Grandfathers and grandchildren working together in the King Island Village *kazgi*. On the left, John Charles Oarloranna, former "chief" of King Island; on the right, Thomas Samnarana, also of King Island; and their grandchildren

Fig. 95. On the right, Bob Omiak of Little Diomede writing the price on the bottom of his small billiken; in the center, Aloysius Pikongonna of King Island reaching for several doves which "Big Mike" Kazingnuk, on the left, has brought into the King Island Village *kazgi* to be priced by Pikongonna and sold

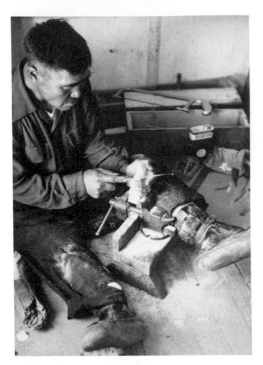

Fig. 96. Pikongonna using a coping saw for the first shaping of the bear illustrated in Figure 64. Note the ivory dust

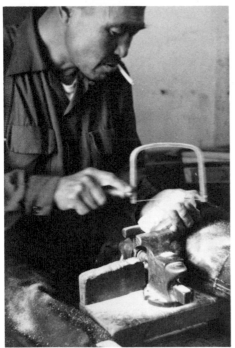

Fig. 97. Further use of the coping saw

Fig. 98. Further use of the coping saw

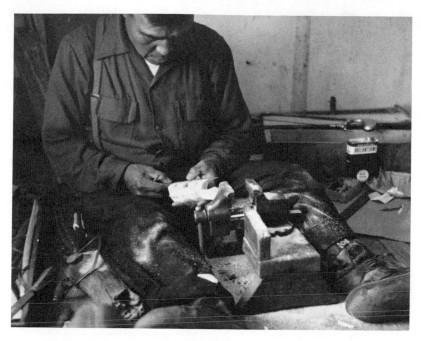

Fig. 99. Pikongonna using a ruler to mark the division of the feet

Fig. 100. Pikongonna using a hack saw of his own manufacture to saw between the feet

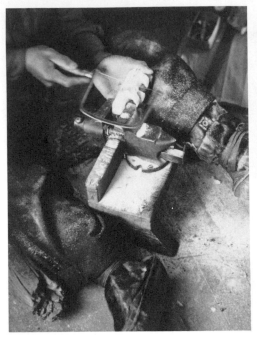

Fig. 101. Pikongonna shaping the first rounded contours of the bear with a coping saw

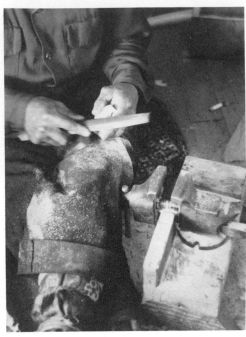

Fig. 102. Pikongonna doing the next shaping with a file after he has rounded the bear with a coping saw

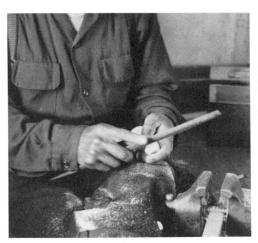

Fig. 103. Further shaping with the file

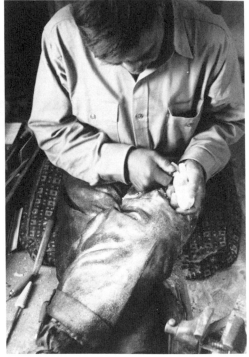

Fig. 104. Pikongonna cutting with a graver into places difficult to reach after the filing is almost completed

Fig. 105. Pikongonna sandpapering the bear after all the sawing and filing have been completed. After this he will polish the bear

Fig. 106. Pikongonna cutting out the mouth and claws of the bear with a graver after the sandpapering and polishing have been completed

Fig. 107. Pikongonna applying hematite to the mouth of the bear, the final step

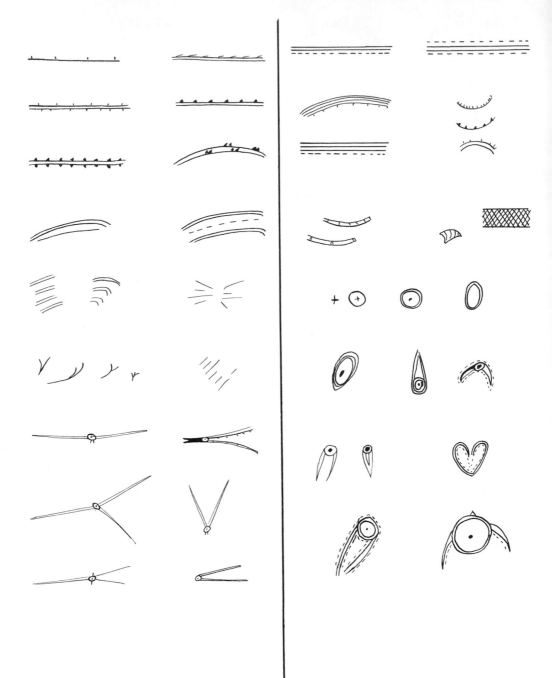

OKVIK COMPONENTS   OLD BERING SEA COMPONENTS

Fig. 108

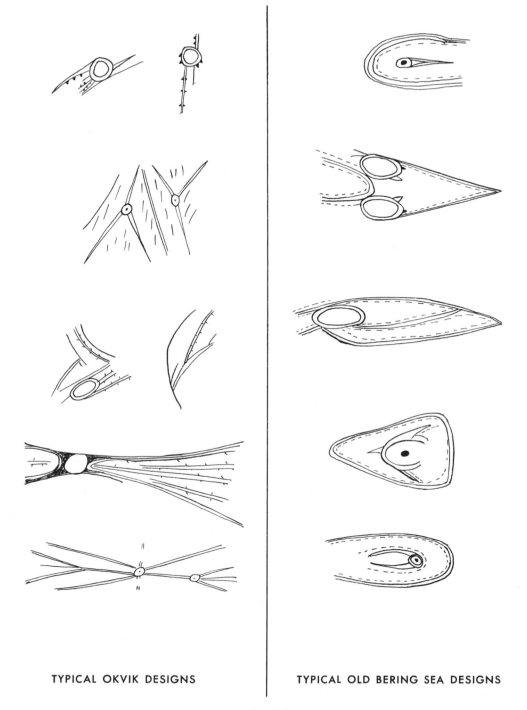

TYPICAL OKVIK DESIGNS | TYPICAL OLD BERING SEA DESIGNS

Fig. 109

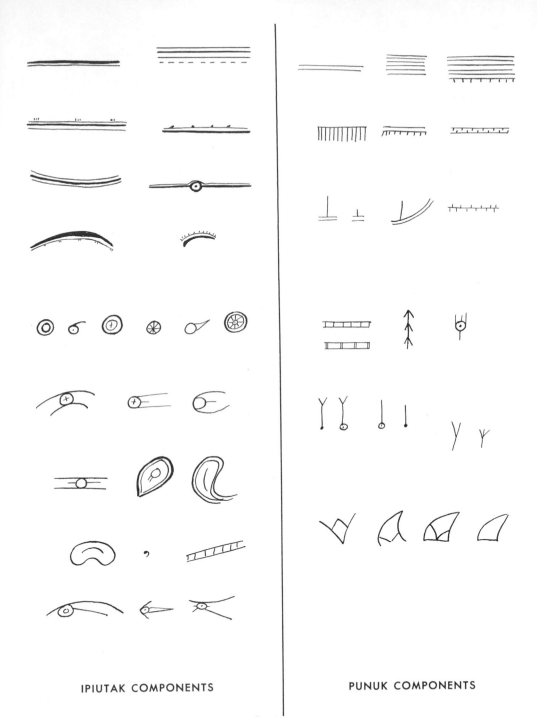

IPIUTAK COMPONENTS   PUNUK COMPONENTS

Fig. 110

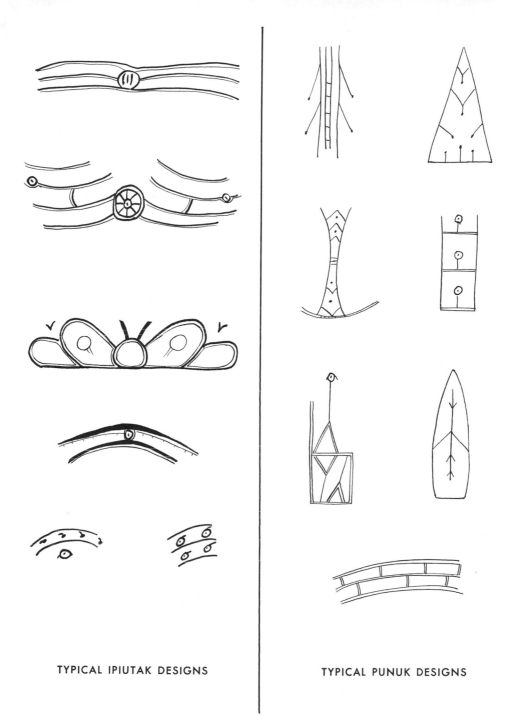

TYPICAL IPIUTAK DESIGNS   TYPICAL PUNUK DESIGNS

Fig. 111

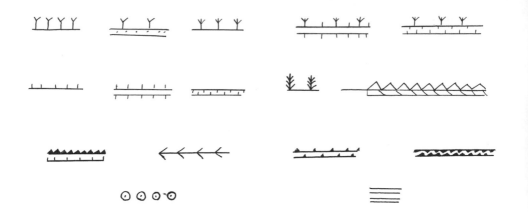

Northern Alaska

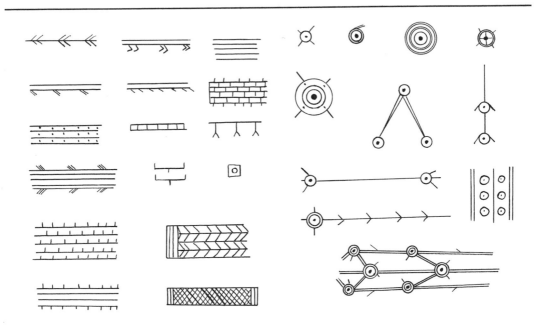

Southwest Alaska

TYPICAL NINETEENTH-CENTURY COMPONENTS AND DESIGNS

Fig. 112

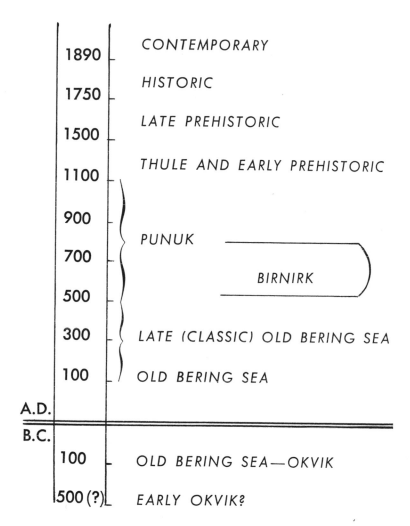

Fig. 113. Eskimo art periods

Ivory splits most easily when it is green or after it has been frozen. However, even old ivory washed out of the beaches has been known to split with the first cut of a knife. Most carvers have learned from experience to identify tusks that might split, but one may still do so when least expected.

Carvers' opinions differ as to the length of time they should dry a tusk before carving, but all agree that it should season for at least two weeks. Some maintain that a month is not too long, and then only small figurines, which will not crack during carving, should be made. Ivory tusks that are to be made into cribbage boards should dry for at least a year.

The carver can cut a tusk in several ways depending on the objects he intends to make, but, in any event, he takes great care from the first to eliminate splitting. When stripping off the rough outer covering he is very careful to adz it from the tip end, not the butt. Some ways of cutting the tusk after adzing are safer than others. For example, there is less danger of the ivory's splitting when the carver saws it into square or rectangular pieces to be used for figurines than when he separates the tusk longitudinally for paper knives.

The carver uses a saw to cut the ivory longitudinally or in cross section for general carving. L. M. Turner, in a letter to Walter Hoffman dated December 26, 1894, said that he had seen southwest Alaskan Eskimos rudely scratch the tusk "with a fragment of quartz, or other siliceous stone, along the length of the tusk until the sharp edge would no longer deepen the groove; the other three sides were scratched or channeled until the pieces of the tusk could be separated. Sometimes this was done by pressure of the hand, or effected by means of a knife-blade-shaped piece of wood, on which was struck a sharp blow, and so skillfully dealt as not to shatter or fracture the piece intended for use. The other side, or slabs, were removed in a similar manner."[5]

One of the present-day carvers about fifty years of age told me that when he was a child he had seen a man make four longitudinal gashes in a tusk with a razor-sharp piece of jade and then drop it to the floor, where it broke into four pieces. However, it is a mystery why these men were using stone tools when metal ones had clearly been in use for several centuries in both the northern and southwest areas.

[5]Walter James Hoffman, *The Graphic Art of the Eskimos* (U.S. National Museum, Annual Report for 1895, Washington, D.C., 1897), p. 774.

An observation made by Lieutenant L. A. Zagoskin about 1843 near St. Michael may partially explain Mr. Turner's report: "Natives have dropped many superstitious ways and adopted Russian customs but still they will never use iron for their spears as they strongly believe the iron which comes from the Russian is unclean from evil spirits."[6] The Eskimos may have wanted to avoid all use of Russian metal if the ivory was to be used in hunting.

Nowadays longitudinal cutting, especially for paper knives, is done in the following manner. After preliminary adzing of the tusk, the carver cuts an incision along its entire length to within a few centimeters of the center with a hack saw. He then makes a second longitudinal cut that meets the first one at the inner edge, resulting in a V-shaped slab, which he removes. Starting from this opening, the carver cuts seven or eight more slabs from the tusk, following the core around. The first wedge, which is usually so thin that it cannot be used, is thrown away, and all subsequent pieces are taken off at once, for the carvers say the tusk is likely to splinter in the future if the core is put away with a section or two remaining.

When a carver wishes to keep ivory for some time before carving, he rubs oil on it, a treatment also recommended for carved objects that are developing cracks. The carver reserves the "best" pieces, that is, those which are very large and without signs of cracking, for carving in the round, using the less desirable pieces for pendants, bracelets, and other small objects. He will discard a figurine immediately if it begins to crack as he works on it. He will then make a smaller figurine from it if the original figurine is large and the crack small; otherwise he usually makes bracelet links.

A carver rarely consents to mend broken ivory, and if he should break off a delicate bird beak or leg during carving he will not glue it back on. A mended spot offends his feeling for perfection, a sentiment that has persisted since the beginning of the industry. Happy Jack received a cribbage board, cleft in the middle, which had traveled three thousand miles so that he could fix it. Rather than spoil the appearance with a ring of glue, he made another one just like it.

About forty years later I encountered a similar situation when I want-

---

[6] L. A. Zagoskin, Account of Pedestrian Journeys in the Russian Possessions in America in 1842, 1843, and 1844 (1847), trans. Mrs. Antoinette Hotovitsky (Typewritten MS, Library of Congress Card No. F907.Z182), p. 64.

ed a head replaced on an animal's body. The carver received the idea of an ivory animal with a glued-on head with such disdain that my only face-saving alternative was to accept a newly carved duplicate of the original one, which had been carved by his father.

All Eskimo carvers consider the mottled core of the walrus tusk both a personal affront and a challenge. It becomes a real problem for the figurine carver because the practice has developed of keeping as much of the core hidden as possible. However, few figurines do not reveal the mottled core somewhere on the surface. A carver cannot predict before he cuts into a tusk whether or not the core, which is a deposit of dentine, will be large or small, but he always hopes that there will be very little. The size of the tusk is no indication of the size of the core, for a very small tusk may have a very large core, and a large one may have only a trace. The core merges into the outside opaque layer without any perceptible transition, such as a fissure or a ridge, but it is often slightly translucent in thin cross section. Tusks that cannot be used for sculptured animals because of the preponderance of core are reserved for billikens and paper knives, which are less highly esteemed.

The fortunes of the inner core have not always been so low. Arabs, Turks, and Persians prized walrus ivory so highly from A.D. 1000 to 1800 that they made sword hilts with the core turned to the outside.[7] Revealing the core in such a manner assured the owners that their hilts would not be mistaken for the more easily obtained and more common elephant ivory.

Sometimes there is a third layer around the outside opaque one, found only at the basal end. This extends a short distance up the tusk, ending in an irregular, undulating line. In contrast to the reluctance with which the carver views the core, he welcomes a large basal area for it becomes a different color white from that of the opaque layer after exposure to the air. The proper placement of these irregular areas often enhances the beauty of a figurine, particularly on the hip of a polar bear or on the breast or at the wing of a bird. In time, these areas usually become chalky white, while the rest of the ivory slowly turns a delicate cream. Occasionally the basal layer turns brown, but no matter which color it becomes the contrast gives the figure an added sculptural effect, espe-

[7]Cammann, "Carvings in Walrus Ivory," pp. 15-16.

cially when the placement has been successful in relation to physical characteristics.[8]

Today, since the demand for carved ivory is greater than ever, the carvers save every useful scrap of ivory. The most recent development in the conservation of ivory is the use of the jagged crystalline substance found in the hollow base of the tusk for cliffs upon which the carver perches a dozen or more exceedingly tiny birds.

[8]This is apparent on the bear, Figure 64. Note also that the mottled core is placed under the bear in a less conspicuous area.

FIVE: The Carver's Tools

LIKE his fellow Eskimos, the carver is a gregarious person who enjoys his work best when in the company of others. This does not mean that he works in the midst of a noisy, frantic crowd. On the contrary, the work is usually done in an atmosphere of calmness and industriousness, a silent fellowship with other carvers.

The *kazgi* in King Island Village exemplifies this atmosphere well. Here, as in the past and on the carvers' own island today, most of the carving is done in the presence of others. At the present time four or five work there at once, all sitting on the floor. Many minutes might elapse without a word being spoken. One man is busily adzing the rough edges from a tusk, another is intent on filing a bear, and still another is smoothing a walrus with sandpaper so vigorously that perspiration streams down his neck (Figs. 94, 95).

The wife of one of the men comes in briefly, says a few low words, and leaves as quietly and quickly as she came. The walrus carver lays down his walrus and lights a corncob pipe. He leans back against the wall, his legs still thrust straight out in front of him, and puffs contentedly for a few minutes before asking the bearmaker a question. They talk quietly in the Eskimo tongue for a long time, the third carver lifting his head occasionally to look at them, but saying nothing.

The bearmaker leaves the *kazgi*, and soon afterward two more men come in, one to take his regular place near his toolbox, and the other

98

just to watch. He has, however, heard some timely bits of gossip in Nome and begins his monologue of events with the two other voices assenting or dissenting now and then, urging him on.

The *kazgi* itself is very large, about fifty feet long and twenty-five feet wide, but has only about fourteen square feet of window space near which the carvers sit to utilize every bit of their meager supply of light. The four small windows at the end opposite the main entrance to the long building do not provide much light even on the most brilliant days because of the northern exposure, and the carvers would not think of using a Coleman lantern until the first of August when a few hours of darkness herald the coming of autumn.

The front door of the *kazgi,* which faces the interminable expanse of Bering Sea, is only a few steps off the road that leads to old Fort Davis (Fig. 5). The front half of the interior is a hodgepodge of outboard motors, paddles, rolled-up skins, and gasoline cans, but in the middle of it all is a wooden picnic table covered with ivory and fur objects. This table, placed squarely in the path of a person entering the building, is the first thing one sees.

I have witnessed many visits of non-Eskimos to the *kazgi,* and most agree that the experience is a rewarding, if unnerving, one. Many of them are, for the first time, meeting head on with members of another race with a strange culture, and, in spite of ideas that they might have had before, they usually leave with admiration and a deep respect for these people at the edge of America.

One day I watched a young man's struggle from the time he entered the *kazgi* until he left. His performance from beginning to end was typical of many visitors who not only are embarrassed by their ignorance of how to behave in such a situation, but are at the same time overly confident because they are white men. The carvers who were working at the back of the building did not even glance at him when he pushed open the squeaky door. Helplessly, he looked at the display table for a long time. He walked around it three times and picked up each object on it at least five. He cleared his throat and held an ivory Canada goose high in the air, hoping for attention, but no salesman rushed to his rescue. There was no sound but the scrape-scrape of the ivory and the quiet voices. I could not encourage him. It was not my *kazgi,* nor was it my ivory. But I knew from experience that those Eskimo voices speaking the

Eskimo language were something he had never before encountered, and that all his resources had failed him.

Finally, he walked to the rear with a bear in his hand and stood looking down at the carvers at work on the floor. He began to gesture in some kind of sign language about the importance of his mission. Then Pikongonna, a friendly man of about fifty, looked up to ask him in excellent English, "You want to buy that?"

The surprised young man answered, "Why, yes. How much is it?"

Pikongonna, with equal promptness, replied, "It's marked right on the bottom—twelve dollars!"

The man acted shocked at the price, and I knew that someone in town who disapproved of the Eskimos had briefed him that he should never pay the price asked.

"That seems terribly high," he said. "How about eight?"

"Twelve is the only price for that," replied Pikongonna, the banker for the group. "Every price that is marked on those ivories is the one that you have to pay. Nothing different."

"I'll tell you what I'll do. I'll make it ten. That is a good price for that," the visitor said with a magnanimous gesture.

Pikongonna sighed deeply and began to rise from his floor mat to return the bear to the table. "That's all right. You don't need to buy it."

The young man paid the full price without further murmur, having learned lessons in patience and in the proper transaction of business among the Eskimos of King Island.

In this *kazgi*, and wherever carvers are at work, their activities are conducted with great seriousness and diligence. Indeed, not only are the processes of creation wearing, but the physical exertion of carving is itself very great. Carving is hard work, and a carver often works himself into a state of perspiration while adzing, sawing, smoothing, or polishing the ivory. Some carvers regard their work as drudgery; they have looked at so much ivory and filed their fingers so often that if offered money or another kind of job they would not hesitate to give up carving. The majority of the men, however, enjoy carving and its constant challenges in spite of the hard labor and low monetary returns. They simply like to carve, and, even when a carver takes a summer job in Nome, he often works ivory in his spare time.

The carvers exhibit creativeness not only in their use of ivory, but also in their manufacturing of tools. Each carver uses a number of tools which he has manufactured or altered to suit his own purposes. The mechanical ingenuity of the Eskimo and his ability to cope with foreign contrivancés came to the attention of the earliest travelers and explorers. In fact, his inventiveness dates back more than two thousand years to when he designed the toggle harpoon head, a device not always accorded its rightful importance in the history of man's inventions. The harpoon head is so constructed that when it imbeds itself in a seal, walrus, or whale, depending on the size of harpoon head, it turns horizontally and thus is prevented from pulling out.

Today the carver usually modifies commercially manufactured tools or makes his own, but he is willing to adopt new tools unaltered if they prove to be more adequate than those he is using. He rarely works with a knife, but shapes most objects with saws, files, and gravers. Only occasionally will one of the older carvers use the age-old "crooked knife" for making a wooden object or shaping an ivory harpoon head which he might sell as a special curio.

There are, however, two aboriginal tools, the adz and the bow drill, for which no substitute has been found. The adz, which the carver uses for stripping off the rough exterior of a tusk, is now made with a steel ax blade hafted to a handle of drift spruce stump (Fig. 90). The bow drill, a unique tool, is so constructed that the user always has one hand free to manipulate the object on which he is working (Fig. 93). The shaft, the upper end of which fits into a mouthpiece held between the teeth, is propelled by a bow made of thong and curved bone. Although the carvers make all parts of the bow drill with great care, they give special attention to the construction of the mouthpiece, which is carefully shaped to fit the driller's mouth. The underside, which must withstand a great deal of friction, is made of syenite. The carvers sometimes substitute iron or some other metal, but because they prefer not to they will spend many hours and even days searching for a suitable piece of the scarce rock.

"It doesn't feel right if we use anything else," they say. "The balance isn't right." Some very adequate mouthpieces have been made with materials other than syenite, however, and probably the real reason for the preference for syenite is the traditional use of it.

The same is true with regard to drill points. Despite the fact that many shapes and sizes of commercial drill points are available, some of the carvers feel that these are inferior to their own, which they usually make of gunny sack needles. They have experimented with, and rejected, commercial hand drills also. They do not use power drills because of the contemporary demand for "handmade" articles; moreover, the King and Little Diomede people have no electricity on their islands.

Hickory, imported from eastern United States, is the favorite wood for drill shafts but spruce, which is gathered as driftwood, runs a close second. The carvers have difficulty finding suitable pieces of spruce although driftwood is often piled high above the tide line on the beaches. They search especially for two parts of the tree, the stump and a slightly bent branch. From the inside bend of the branch they fashion snowshoes, drumsticks, and drum frames as well as bow drill shafts. From the stump they make snowglasses, masks, spoons, and dishes.

They consider whale jawbone the best material for the bow itself but often use whale rib instead. These are boiled until soft and pliable.

When a commercially made file is used as a file it is not altered by the carvers, but even that tool has not escaped their penchant for alteration. They use it as raw material for a favorite three-cornered graver and for a special scraper. The former is made from the pointed end of the file, which is detached and mounted in a well-carved ivory handle, and the latter is made from the lengthwise edges of the file. Even when the carvers buy commercial straight-ended gravers they usually add a personal touch—a new handle, for instance, or an addition to an existing handle.

They make a large number of gravers from table and butcher knives (Fig. 91). A peculiar local variety with a sharp point made at right angles to the vertical axis of the blade could perhaps more rightly be called a burin. The carvers keep their gravers razor sharp for engraving as well as for cutting out areas difficult to reach. To the good artist the sharpness of his tools is indispensable, but this is something which takes maturity to appreciate. One carver said that when he was young he resented every minute spent sharpening his tools, but now he finds it almost as enjoyable as carving. Each carver has a rectangular toolbox, often equipped with a padlock, in which he keeps his tools. Only one of the island carvers possesses an old pre-European oval driftwood box with beautifully inlaid geometric pieces of ivory. He reputedly has refused "lots and lots of money" for it.

The carver will not hesitate to loan one of his tools. There is little lending, however, because each carver has developed a kit of tools for his own carving needs. When he does borrow a tool it usually is a specialized one which he rarely uses.

The two instruments used for sculpturing are the file and the saw. The most commonly used files are a twelve-inch flat one, a six-inch half-rod, and a six-inch single-cut fine file. For engraving, the straight-ended graver is used almost exclusively. Each carver has a number of them in different widths. This is important particularly for making of a conventionalization called the "zigzag," the width of which is determined by the width of the graver. The zigzag is used for two purposes, the representation of density in two-dimensional engravings and the simulation of feathers on sculptured birds (Figs. 62, 67).

The making of the zigzag appears very simple in the hands of a competent carver, but a novice can hardly dent the ivory without a great deal of practice. To make the zigzag the carver first places the graver in the ivory to make a straight line. With one end of it kept in place, he lifts the opposite end to a point a very short way from the end of the horizontal line. This results in a slanting line originating from the end of the graver which had remained in place. This line and the horizontal line touching it at one end look like a V on its side. The end of the graver that had just been lifted now stays anchored in place while the other one is moved to a point opposite the end of the first slanting line, making a line parallel to the original horizontal line. The result is a Z. The carver makes dozens of these without a break in the continuity and does it so swiftly, rocking his graver back and forth from end to end, that it seems as if he hardly touches the ivory. When he desires unusual density he makes all the lines very close together. When a blackening agent is applied to these, the result is almost a solid black.

The carver uses both hack saws and coping saws, the former for sawing large tusks into blocks, and the latter for the initial shaping of an animal. Although some of the carvers use commercial saws, they always favor those which they have manufactured. For instance, Pikongonna's hack saw, of which he is extremely proud, is constructed of bone, ivory, wood, wire, and a steel blade. One of the Diomede Island carvers regularly makes his own coping saw blades from phonograph springs. When they do use commercially made saws, they prefer a hack saw blade with sixteen points to an inch, and a coping saw with a fine number five blade.

The carvers have invented two tools especially for present-day carving: a two-pronged holder for holding bracelet links during engraving, smoothing, and polishing; and a scraper for eradicating file marks. However, one of the carvers told me, "We never get the file marks all off; there's always some left somewhere." And then he added cryptically, "But when white people try to carve the things we do, they try to take all of them off."

The holder consists of an ivory handle into which are inserted two wires as far apart as the holes for elasticized string in the bracelet itself are to be. To make the scraper, the carver must destroy a file, which he sharpens the entire length of one or both of its longitudinal sides.

Other tools besides the file which the carvers use unaltered in contemporary carving are the table vise, which is used constantly when sawing; the tap and die for threading the ivory for necklace clasps; a watchmaker's magnifying glass; a hand vise; and a circular brush, the latter two used principally by carvers of the billiken (a good-luck piece). The carvers do not use the magnifying glass as much as they did in the early days when extremely fine and exact copying and engraving were a high art.

A carver's miscellaneous equipment usually includes a bleached-skin thimble and a driftwood stump. The thimble was formerly a flat, shield-like piece of heavy parchment, but now it is often shaped like a steel thimble. This is used during filing, for, although the majority of the carvers are very adept in using files, they sometimes miscalculate in their speedy operations and file their fingers instead of the ivory.

Almost every carver uses a small driftwood stump to support the ivory while adzing, sawing, and, often, engraving. This simple support competes favorably with a vise in popularity, and the carver will keep one for years until the top is disfigured by thousands of adz and saw marks. He also makes extensive use of his mukluks to support the ivory. A right-handed carver usually steadies the ivory on the right mukluk, which he rests on top of the left one. The inside edge of the left leg is then used as a secondary prop for the hand holding the ivory.

All carvers follow the same basic step-by-step procedure in the carving of the majority of objects. The following descriptions of the carving of two typical objects, a large bear and a very small billiken, will illustrate the role of various tools in ivory sculpture. Figures 96 through 107 show the steps in the carving of the bear pictured in Figure 64.

The first step in the making of any object is the trimming of the tusk with the adz. An experienced ivory worker takes dainty bites out of the hard ivory with the adz as easily as if it were coconut meat. After he has trimmed the tusk neatly, he cuts it into square or rectangular pieces, each section representing the approximate size of the animal or object he will make from it. As a rule all figurines, including large billikens, are begun in this manner.

Usually the carver hurriedly places a few pencil lines on the block of ivory as guides and, on this basis, cuts out a few chunks of ivory from the block with a hack saw. The result is a blocklike animal, with four slabs of ivory representing the two front and two rear legs, and a rectangular piece, the neck. For further refinement the carver uses a coping saw next, referring to his pencil marks for the animal's outline.

By now the carver has produced all the essential parts of the bear—four legs, neck, and head—but it is scarcely recognizable because of its chocky angularity. The recognizable animal emerges as the carver uses a succession of files in increasing degrees of fineness. Sometimes during the course of filing he cuts out the ears and mouth with a graver and makes holes for eyes, which he will inlay with contrasting material of ivory or baleen after he has used the last fine file. When carvers do not make inset eyes, they gouge out a hole with a graver instead, coloring it with graphite.

To fit the inset material into the hole, the carver cuts one end to the approximate size of the eye and tapers the other. He then inserts the tapered end into the eye as tightly as possible, paring it off flush with the ivory. Inset eyes are held in the ivory through friction, but the flat inlaid bracelet pieces are glued with cement. During the nineteenth century, wood and even pieces of rock were used as inlays.

To make a bear twelve and a half centimeters long, the foregoing steps would take about twelve hours, the cutting and filing consuming about three-fourths of that time. After completing the filing, the carver sandpapers it with new grade three sandpaper, then subsequently with reused and and worn-out pieces until the ivory is smooth. He then applies a metal polish and vigorously polishes the bear with a cloth until it gleams. After that, he cuts out the claws and mouth, applying graphite for the claws and hematite for the mouth after the polishing so that the color will not rub out.

The steps in making a bird are very similar to those for the bear, except that the carver usually begins with a coping saw instead of a hack saw. After all the fine finishing and polishing have been done, the bird is covered with the conventional zigzag to represent feathers. The carver then rubs graphite over all of the incised places, removing the excess with a cloth and fingers. If India ink is used, it is poured over the entire object and clings to the incisions, while the remainder is easily wiped off the smooth ivory.

A small billiken three centimeters high takes only forty-five minutes to make in contrast to the twelve hours for a bear twelve and a half centimeters long. The carver prepares a tusk differently when he wishes to make nothing but the small and highly stylized billikens from it. He divides it into longitudinal pieces the width and depth of the proposed billiken instead of into chunks. To make a billiken three centimeters high, the carver cuts a piece four centimeters in length from one of the longitudinal pieces which he holds in a vise (Fig. 92). He then clamps a hand vise on the extra centimeter of ivory and holds it in this manner during the entire carving. The billiken is fashioned almost entirely by filing, the file biting into the ivory with speedy decisiveness. The carver uses a graver only to cut under the chin and to indicate fingers, the fringe, and the small vertical line in front. Even the ears are shaped with the file. When the finished billiken is to be used as a pendant, the carver drills a hole from one side of the head to the other, using the cut-off blade of a jackknife to enlarge it. He uses a finer file for further shaping after he has sandpapered and polished the figure. Then he usually deepens the fringes with a graver and cleans out the residual pieces of ivory with a brush.

Contemporary carvers not only continue to regard ivory as a superior raw material but now prize it also as a rare one. Their own high evaluation has been added to by the old European and Oriental assessment of ivory. Some of their criticisms of carved objects stem from this acquired evaluation that "ivory is ivory," as one carver put it. "We have learned that it is a rare thing."

All Eskimo cultures, however, have apparently regarded ivory with unusual interest. With few exceptions, the early pieces of carved ivory were well finished and polished. The carvers must have felt that it was, indeed, a rare material, or at least that it had a rare quality which impelled them to bring out all the beauty of the raw material. They must always have enjoyed working the medium as much as viewing the objects that emerged from it.

The harshest criticisms of the carvers arise when objects are over-decorated. "Ivory should never be covered up because it is expensive in history," is the way a carver expressed it.

Still another said, "If ivory is painted it looks like poor wood which has *had* to be painted."

The value of colored old walrus ivory has increased appreciably more than new ivory. In the old days the Eskimos regarded it as nothing more than another raw material, and it was rarely used because of the abundance of fresh ivory. But now it has acquired a glamorous new role in a world that seeks the rare and savors the unique. Collectors are not alone in their admiration of these beautiful pieces, for the carvers themselves have a great appreciation for the unusual combinations of many colors and striations often found in this ivory. Whenever they make ornaments for themselves they are likely to be from a choice piece of the old ivory, although bracelets have only recently become popular; they prefer commercial "costume jewelry." Personal ivory decorations in old Eskimo times were confined to earrings, belt buckles, and baubles for the hair.

The carvers strive constantly to keep objects "handmade" because they perceive that this is one of the intrinsic values of the Eskimo-carved ivories. Their awareness of this value has been heightened during the last two decades when a general revival of, and interest in, the folk arts appeared everywhere. However, the carver is often disturbed by this trend because he feels that it has been a deterrent to some potentially fine machine-made goods.

"The trouble is," one of the carvers told me, "they [the customers] will buy even poor stuff if they know it is 'handmade.' "

He was right to a certain extent, for a few unperceptive purchasers become carried away not only by the obviously handmade quality of the poorer pieces but by their low cost. In recent years, however, such objects have taken longer to sell than the very good ones. The customers' discrimination shows that the majority are usually more than souvenir-seekers; they also are collectors of art.

The emphasis on retaining the "handmade" characteristics, which has led to the disdain of electric machinery, has had other results that are slightly irrational. For example, some of the carvers will not use India ink to fill in engravings or to indicate anatomical details. One of them told me, "We have learned a lot from the whites. They tell us that that looks artificial."

Thus the carvers, particularly those from King Island, use lead pencil or cigarette ash, both of which are derived from the same commercial market as the India ink. The majority of the Diomede Island people, however, prefer to use India ink for lips, eyes, whiskers, and claws. Graphite put into claws always "looks dirty," is the common consensus among the carvers. The chief alternative to India ink, therefore, is to leave the claws uncolored, and this is one of the diagnostic features of Pikongonna's very fine bears.

Asiatic graphite was probably traded to American Eskimos by Asiatic Eskimos in the course of the extensive trade carried on across the Bering Strait during the nineteenth century. Nordenskiöld, who visited the Bering Strait area in 1879, said that he was given a number of pieces of graphite on the Asiatic side of Bering Strait.[1] At about the same time the Alaskan Eskimos were also using other materials for filling in the engraved portions of their hunting tallies and tusks. Lucien Turner said that they often used charcoal from burned grass which they mixed with oil,[2] and Nelson reported that they used charcoal or gunpowder mixed with blood.[3]

[1]A.E. Nordenskiöld, *The Voyage of the Vega round Asia and Europe* (New York: Macmillan and Co., 1882), p. 576.

[2]Walter James Hoffman, *The Graphic Art of the Eskimos* (U.S. National Museum, Annual Report for 1895, Washington, D.C., 1897), p. 790.

[3]Edward William Nelson, *The Eskimo about Bering Strait* (Bureau of American Ethnology, Annual Report, Vol. XVIII, Part I, 1899), p. 198.

Nowadays the carver moistens both the graphite and cigarette ash with water or saliva before application, rubs it on the ivory with his fingers, and wipes off the excess with a cloth.

The carvers have also developed the viewpoint that nothing but black color should be used for contrast in two-dimensional engravings. Although a few carvers have begun to use red pencil for the mouths of birds and animals, the majority of carvers frown on this, preferring to search for hematite when they need red color.

The carvers are also inconsistent in their attitude toward the use of machinery. For example, although it is taboo to use power tools for the carving of animals, this does not apply to the making of beads. The opinion among carvers is that beadmaking by hand is the most tedious of all work. To make a bead the carver drills a hole in a small piece of ivory, inserts a nail or a piece of wire, and, with only a file, wears the piece down to the size and shape of bead he desires. As the work progresses, the file turns the bead swiftly around, producing a great deal of friction on the hand and fingers. It is not surprising, then, that when the Eskimos were introduced to the sewing machine they converted dozens of them into lathes for making beads. This use of a machine may be considered separately from the power category, however, for the lathe not only is a product of the carvers' own ingenuity, but is usually hand-operated.

The attitude of the customers is, however, the principal reason for the acceptance of machine-made beads, for they rarely give a thought to the creativeness involved in making a bead. They are prone to think of a bead as nothing more than an unimaginative oval that springs automatically from the carver's tools. This conception would not persist if they could hear the criticisms of various beads by the carvers and the nostalgic reminiscences of kinds that are never made now.

Beads have been made in many shapes, but the most famous are those of a teardrop design made twenty-five or thirty years ago. For these the carver used an unusually colored mammoth ivory with a light area merging into a darker one. To get the effect of a drop of water about to burst, he made the narrow end of each bead of the light color and the rounded end of the darker.

A few years ago square- and rectangular-shaped beads appeared in Nome, presumably from St. Lawrence Island or possibly East Cape, Siberia (Fig. 81). The carvers in Nome thought at first that this was a very lazy kind of work—beads with square corners! But, on second thought, it occurred to them that perhaps the maker of these had had a "new idea," which might "work out" after all.

The carvers have such great respect for handmade beads that they sometimes carry it to undue lengths. For example, if two bracelets, one with beautifully carved animal links and the other nothing but a series of hand-carved beads, were presented to them for appraisal, the bead bracelet would be the overwhelming favorite—it is the one they "like best," it is the "better," or is "better carved."

Before World War II one of the carvers used a commercial electric lathe for beads and an electric drill instead of the bow drill for making holes through square and rectangular bracelet links. With this combination he could finish six or more bracelets a day, increasing his production even more when he finally added a power polisher. Because of a growing market at the newly opened Marks Field across the Snake River from Nome, he sold the bracelets as fast as he could make them until the demand diminished. Turning then to the merchants in town, he discovered that they did not want "machine-made" goods glutting the market. One of them told him, furthermore, that if he used machinery he would have "bad luck all the rest of his life," and the carver, faced with a future full of potential misfortune as well as a present without a market, returned to carving by hand.

Retail dealers in Nome have been known to do more than capitalize on superstition. A carver told me in 1955 that "I was promised jail if I sold any more carvings to the army boys," and because he knew so little of the law and had been intimidated for so long by the dealers he was more than willing to conform in order to safeguard his only source of income.

SIX: What the Carver Makes

W HEN a carver begins to adz a tusk he has two questions in mind: what am I going to carve, and how can I use my ivory to the best advantage?

There are numerous factors that determine the objects a carver will make at a certain time, but the basic ones are the size of the tusk and the amount of ivory he possesses. Sculpture from a walrus tusk is of necessity small, and it is probably for this reason alone that no large art pieces are found in archeological sites. Carvers today would not be averse to making larger objects of wood, but, as previously mentioned, they find few solid and sturdy driftwood stumps or limbs.

It has been suggested that ivory carvings were made in small sizes for the sake of portability, but the Eskimos in this rich hunting area were only seminomadic, living in comparatively permanent villages. They were also known to make huge, untransportable "statues." The best-known one, a face carved out of a big driftwood stump, was located on Big Diomede Island. Carved a hundred years ago by an influential man named Aneuna, it received the first game of each season presented by the inhabitants of the island.

A man carves small objects today, however, for other reasons. For example, if he is short of ivory he will make only bracelets, billikens, or very small animals, but not large animals, paper knives, or birds. Paper knives, in particular, waste a large amount of ivory.

Using a tusk to best advantage also means making items that bring in the most income for the amount of ivory used plus the amount of time consumed in carving them. For instance, if a carver makes bracelets and billikens from a tusk these would net him about four times as much as if he made a cribbage board but probably would take him twenty times as long to make. However, if a carver has little ivory he has no alternative but to make smaller pieces.

To get "quick money" a carver makes a cribbage board, which he considers the lowest priced commodity in relation to the amount of ivory used. In the summer the King Island carvers make cribbage boards only when the supply on the display table has diminished. They never keep a large number on hand as do some of the curio shops in Nome.

Another determinant of what the carver will make is the condition of the ivory—its tendency to split and the amount of core. If the tusk on which he is working splits he will have to make small objects or beads and links from the resultant pieces. If the ivory has too much core he cannot make the larger sculptured animals such as bears, walruses, and birds unless he can hide it satisfactorily. There is no aversion to using the core for billikens or paper knives, or for bracelet links if a thin layer of the opaque ivory remains on the top surface.[1] The carver might use slightly cracked pieces, but never the mottled core, for engraving.

The carvers, with the exception of one or two men on St. Lawrence Island, do not carve delicate objects. They feel that the danger of breakage during carving is too great, and, in accordance with their practice of discarding broken objects, they hesitate to undertake this risk. Moreover, the making of delicate pieces necessitates slow and painstaking work, and under present conditions of low prices the carver feels compelled to make things that do not take long to carve. In the earlier days, when carvings had not reached their present economic importance, many more objects of a more fragile nature were made.

The delicate carving of St. Lawrence Island consists mainly of paper-thin filigree ivory necklaces, which Tungyan originated in the 1920's, and which have since been made by only two other men.[2] These are usually acquired as works of art rather than as articles to be worn, and they must be handled with special care after purchase. It is said that

[1] In Figure 77 the interspersing links were chosen deliberately for the beautiful mottled effect.
[2] Several exquisite necklaces made by Tungyan and collected by Otto William Geist are in the University of Alaska Museum.

unless they are kept flattened under pressure or immersed in an oily substance they have a tendency to warp.

Another important guidepost for the carver in what he is to make is the demand of the customer at a particular time. Likes and dislikes of collectors have changed throughout the years, and an item of immense popularity thirty years ago may collect dust in a shop today. The carver is kept posted on present popularity and need for objects by both the Alaska Native Arts and Crafts Clearing House in Juneau and the local stores.

With the carvers bounded on one side by the size and quantity of their ivory and on the other by the whims of the market, it might appear that originality is at a premium. Although this is often true, carvers throughout the years have tried many new kinds of objects and decorative motifs. If these proved successful within the limits of the desires of the purchasers, they became marketable objects. Originators usually are those who do not have to depend on the immediate sale of their products, but, even at that, they are few in number. This will be discussed more completely later. It should be clear, however, that a carver with unlimited amounts of ivory would be enabled to move within a more varied world of creation than one with only a tusk or two.

In spite of the restrictions of both the market and the size of the ivory, a man will not carve anything that he does not like to carve. Best-liked objects are bears or birds; the least-liked, billikens. If there is nothing else for sale on the King Island *kazgi* table, there will be birds.

Birds have been favorites in all phases of Eskimo life. (For examples of birds in Eskimo art, see Figures 13, 19, 21, 22, 28, 31, 33, 36, 62, 63, and 67.) Bird tales abound in Eskimo mythology, and the beautiful eagle episodes are among the most important of Eskimo oral literature. Concrete examples of bird motifs are found in archeological ivory carving. There are the Old Bering Sea formalized birds on harpoon heads and harpoon foreshafts, and the Thule people's flocks of flat-bottomed birds which they used in a game, *Tingmiujaq*. In the collections brought back to the museums in the nineteenth century, bird motifs are particularly numerous on the complicated masks of the southwest Alaskan Eskimo. Accounts of festivals and ceremonies always include myriad references to bird objects that occupied prominent places in the building during the activities, but unfortunately the meaning of these birds and their use. both on masks and in the festivities, have rarely been ascertained.

Birds, or parts of birds such as feathers, did miraculous things for human beings in legendary accounts. They enabled them to fly in the air, or to go as fast as an arrow in a kayak. The eagle and the brant goose also told the Eskimos how to dance two of their most important dances, the Eagle Dance and the Red Fox Dance. Not only did the eagle tell them how to prepare for the dance, but he ordered them to make a box drum, the pounding of which is the beating of his heart.

The snowbird in the Bering Strait area is a creator who made a man when there was only emptiness. This man in turn created four more representing the directions, North, South, East, and West, each of whom created the remainder of the population. Pikongonna told me that he likes to make the snowbird better than any other bird.

Some of the carvers steadfastly refuse to carve billikens, which they consider monotonous and boring. Pikongonna, who can be called one of the best carvers of all time, said that he had carved two or three billikens "one time."

"I never made any more of them after that," he added.

There is a great deal of cooperation and unselfishness in the use of ideas and tools within the King Island group and the Diomede Island group, but much less between the two. The Eskimo of today likes to think that cooperativeness and unselfishness are special characteristics of his culture. He believes it to be the antithesis of the culture of the white man, which he sees as riddled with uncooperative and selfish aspects. Actually, the Eskimo culture was no less cooperative than most isolated societies in which altruistic efforts were needed for the sustenance of individual pursuits. The lack of cooperation between certain Eskimos of King and Diomede islands, not readily apparent or admitted, is a continuation of the typical intergroup rivalries that have marked Eskimo history so clearly.

Unlimited cooperation and help are given within the group not only in carving but in all areas of life. As in prewhite days, food is shared, clothing distributed, and labor given to all who are worthy of it. In earlier times if a man misappropriated food, was extremely lazy, or committed offenses against the general rules, he would have been ostracized, possibly to the point of excommunication from the village. Today, if an able-bodied man refused to contribute his share to the group, but nevertheless needed food or aid, it would be made clear to him that he would receive nothing unless he did his part.

Ideas and designs are universally used throughout the entire carving territory of Bering Strait. An originator of a design or object does not have exclusive ownership just because he thought of it first. Others are always free to copy. However, in actual practice a new idea may continue to be the exclusive property of the originator for various reasons. For example, very often another carver will not adopt a new design or make a new object because he is suspicious of its potential success on the market. Sometimes a carver will wait months or years to gauge the success of an innovation. Moreover, a carver may not care to add another object to his repertoire for, although versatility is highly prized, competence is acquired through a constant practice of a limited number of items. If a carver has found a few specialties that he not only carves well but has no trouble selling, he will confine himself to these.

Another restraint for the common use of all carving ideas is the reluctance of a group to adopt a specialty carving of another. When only one group adopts a new object or design it might appear that it is theirs exclusively. But the exclusiveness is created not by the group that does the carving, but by those who do not. Thus, in spite of their idealized way of looking at themselves as well as actual instances of cooperation and unselfishness, underlying currents of rivalry erupt in various manners.

The Diomede Islanders do not often make the bird figurines for which the King Islanders are famous, and the latter rarely make the dog-team or bear-head bracelets of the Diomeders. A mere general rivalry, however, is not the only reason why each island group continues its own specialties. Two other reasons, neither related to the carver as artist or to the finished product as a piece of art, are apparent.

Skillful carving of small pieces is no matter of pride to a carver, although in the past extremely small carvings were often sought by collectors. Birds and large animals require large pieces of raw ivory, and when carvers are short of ivory they make only small billikens or bracelets. Ivory shortages occur more frequently among the Diomede Islanders than among the King Islanders, who would rather not carve if compelled to make little things.

Another important reason why the King Island carvers do not make animal bracelets, at least during the summer carving season, is the low price the Diomede Islanders ask for them. One of the King Island men said that he could not afford to carve a bracelet for less than twenty dollars, "so when the Diomede Islanders keep the price at twelve dollars I'm not going to carve just to sell at that price."

The selling of carved ivory is of primary importance to the carver, but it is not so important that he will take the first price offered him, and the best carvers will not sell pieces that do not measure up to their own standards.

The carvings sold in the King Island *kazgi* are priced by Pikongonna, usually on the basis of length. For instance, bears usually sell for two dollars an inch for the best ones, possibly less for poorer ones. No customer has succeeded in lowering one of these prices through bargaining. One price is set, and Pikongonna, speaking for the entire King Island group, sticks to it. However, if a piece has lain on the table for two or three weeks without being sold, the price is lowered voluntarily by Pikongonna with the consent of the carver.

The concept of fixed prices for goods has long been a part of this same tradition. In 1906 Harrison wrote, "The Eskimo has one price for his wares, and it would be extraordinary circumstance that would cause him to take a lower price,"[3] and in 1826 Beechey found among the Eskimos a principle of "never raising or lowering their prices."[4]

The Eskimo's lack of salesmanship has been known to bother outsiders who deal with the carvers, as we have seen. The carvers take a passive role not only in selling their ivory, but in selling other things, too. I once witnessed the sale of a polar bear skin in which the only salesmen appeared to be the skins themselves. A number of men stood at hand to help unroll a cumbersome skin for a woman customer. Since it did not please her, she asked to see another.

The men were extremely reluctant to unroll another one, but they did so without a word. When both skins were stretched on the floor, she asked which was the better one, and the men, silent until then, agreed that both were fine. Thereupon she asked that a third be unrolled, and again the whole group surveyed the skins without a sound.

[3]E.S. Harrison, *Nome and the Seward Peninsula* (Seattle, 1905), p. 29.

[4]F.W. Beechey, *Narrative of a Voyage to the Pacific and Beering's Strait, 1825-1828* (London, 1831), Part I, p. 289.

The woman seemed eager to have the men advise her which skin she should buy, but, when they did answer her numerous queries about the respective qualities of the skins, all they said was, "Any of them are good; they're all good."

Carvers who are not affiliated with the King Island *kazgi* sell their goods regularly through three channels: retail stores; the Alaska Native Arts and Crafts Clearing House, with headquarters in Juneau; and individuals who collect ivory or buy it for future resale.

The first two have set prices, and the carver has the choice of selling or refusing to sell. The third group has an opportunity to buy when the carver feels that the price offered by the first two groups is insufficient. Individuals sometimes order a specific number of items at a stated price, always paying the carver after the pieces are delivered. The personnel of Marks Field were one of the best outlets of this kind until the closing of that installation.

Even when a carver sells to an individual at a cheaper price, it is not appreciably lower. It is only when all other attempts have proved fruitless, in a moment of despair, or, occasionally, when in need of a drink of liquor, that he will sell the ivory at a reduced price. Selling ivory in this manner is frowned upon by the King Islanders although a few of the carvers do it if they have an excess of carved ivory before leaving Nome for their island home in October.

The King Islanders recently inaugurated one exception to their rule of selling their goods at a standard rate by trading with the icebreaker that sometimes stops at their ice-locked island in the middle of the long, dark winter. This occurrence takes on the aspect of an old-fashioned trading fair, for the carvers exchange their ivory for merchandise instead of money, and they say that they have the "best fun of the year," in spite of the fact that they lose money with every transaction.

One carver told me, "Even when they want to give us cash we want to trade. When that happens and they are almost out of their own supplies they go to the store [the cooperative store on the island] and come back loaded down with boxes of cigarettes, laughing, and saying they're ready to trade now!" He also said that he carves bracelets during the winter in anticipation of the icebreaker's visit, refusing to sell them in the summer in competition with the Diomede carvers.

The carvers' preoccupation with the prices they receive for their goods is understandable when it is remembered that a carver can earn, at the most, only eight or nine hundred dollars a year. With the high cost of living in Nome, this is comparable to an income of three or four hundred dollars in the rest of the United States. There is little justification for customers' complaints of "high prices in ivory" when they buy ivory direct from the carver in Nome; the prices would seem reasonable enough if the customers considered the amount of time and the ivory put into each piece by the carver. For instance, in my timing of the making of dozens of kinds of objects, the highest hourly wage approached $1.25 an hour, and the average was just under a dollar.

"And don't forget," one of the carvers pointed out, "you are getting the ivory for nothing."

SEVEN: Innovations and Their History

SEVERAL kinds of carvings have had a long reign of popularity, the cribbage board since the beginning of contemporary carving, and the billiken and animal figurines since the first decade. Bird figurines and elasticized bracelets were relative latecomers, appearing in the early 1920's but still popular now after thirty years. Many other kinds have come and gone, following the whims and fleeting demands of the customers.

The sudden breaking with the old tradition of carving, intensified by the omnivorous requests of the souvenir seekers, made the first years of the industry exploratory ones. The carvers kept their old techniques and products as long as they could, on the one hand, but on the other were forced almost at once to make things they had never heard of, such as salt and pepper shakers, cane handles, and gavels. This period of unlimited new ideas and the carvers' willingness to give them concreteness created a heterogeneity of products at the outset. There was no tentative, timid exploration; everything was tried and done so well that sometimes first attempts were never improved upon.

That period of feverish invention has ended, and the industry has attained a general sophistication and excellence that were present sporadically in the early days but were not characteristic of it as a whole. The trend over the years has been toward the creation of artistic objects of more universal appeal and of more intrinsic esthetic value.

In the early years, popular ephemera of the period were immortalized in ivory: kewpie dolls, "September Morn" of the White Rock bottle, the "potty doll," watch fobs, and napkin rings. Along with shaggy-haired foxes on umbrella handles, wide-winged eagles on gavels, and fancy toothpicks, these have gone out of production with little likelihood of revival.

Fortunately there are still a few carvers living today who remember the early-day carving from first-hand experience, but the majority of them make objects of whose history they are ignorant. This ignorance is a result mainly of the free borrowing of ideas from unknown or forgotten originators, particularly if the borrower lived in a distant village or had only recently moved to Nome.

The Eskimo carvers lay no stress on remembering the history of the objects they make; consequently there is little reason for them to remember the originator of any particular one. It is doubtful whether credit has always been given to the rightful originator, for no records have been kept except in the carvers' memories. And, although credit may be given to only one person, actually several persons might have participated in the original development of an object.

The majority of contemporary pieces have resulted from dealers' or customers' suggestions, a lesser number from the imagination of the carvers. This does not mean, however, that the carvers have no originality, although its development has not been nurtured even among themselves since the beginning of the contemporary phase of carving. Originality has been de-emphasized for two reasons. In the first place, the old Eskimo art was channeled to utilitarian and religious objects as well as toys which have been supplanted by foreign articles. The Eskimos seldom make anything for their own use nowadays, and they cherish old wooden buckets, trays, and dolls of eighty years ago as heirlooms.

In the second place, the carver was compelled to make objects that fitted into the carving scheme no matter how unknown or foreign they were to him. At first the Eskimos were successful in selling copies of their own cultural appurtenances, for example, drag handles and needlecases, but soon the customers were demanding display objects made as "originals" by the Eskimos.

Cribbage boards were the first definite departure from traditional carving, both in form and design. Happy Jack's first cribbage board,

made about 1892, was so successful that Eskimos of the King and Diomede islands were trading them to whalers and other sailing men before
tents had blossomed on the bleak shore near Cape Nome after the gold
strike. John A. Cook, captain of a whaling ship in the Bering Strait, is
one of the few who noted the early carving of these Eskimos. On June
29, 1898, just three months before gold was discovered on Anvil Creek,
he stopped at King Island where he writes, "The natives are very ingen-
ious in tattooing ivory, and many cribbage-boards are made from the
tusks of walrus."[1]

Two years later, on May 24, 1900, he stopped at Little Diomede Island, about which he comments: "The boots that are made here are
superior to any that can be had, and their tattooing of ivory is indeed
artistic, being the best of any of the Eskimos."[2]

Like so many of the Eskimo-carved objects, the cribbage boards cannot be described adequately in a few words. They have been made in
all sizes and decorated with an astonishing variety and juxtaposition of
subjects both carved and engraved. The expanse of ivory on the large
"boards" gave the carver unlimited freedom for the engraving of his
often incongruous mixture of Eskimo and foreign subjects within one
framework. Favorite scenes now are typically Eskimo: dog teams, human
figures in various occupational aspects, and illustrative figures of typical
arctic animals and birds (Figs. 54, 55, 75). Present-day carvers rarely
engrave old-time favorites of the American flag, roses, and old American
scenes from magazines because they have discovered that the consumer,
in buying from them, likes to feel that he has purchased something
"Eskimo-like."

A style of cribbage board that departs from the original development
was created in the late 1920's on Nunivak Island (Figs. 68-75). These
tusks, which are unique among Eskimo carvings, are deeply sculptured
with complexly intertwined animals. Nunivak Island was essentially a
stronghold of excellent wood painting and mask making, but, when the
Lomen brothers began raising reindeer there, they imported raw ivory
to encourage the Eskimos in an industry that already had proved popular in Nome.

This type of carving, which was the invention of one carver, has been
restricted to this island. Carvers farther north have heard about it but

[1]John A. Cook, *Pursuing the Whale* (New York: Houghton Mifflin Co., 1926), p. 151.
[2]*Ibid.*, p. 209.

have not imitated it. The principal animals used in this intricate concept are foxes and walruses, the eyes invariably inset with baleen and the whiskers made in the shape of a comma, a conventionalization that has never been found archeologically in this region but is present in the Ipiutak material, about nine hundred years old, from Kotzebue. The majority of the tusks are carved solely for ornamental display, however, for the carver is often unwilling to disturb the continuity of animals for the inclusion of the utilitarian cribbage "board."

The billiken, one of the least imaginative objects made by the carvers, is also their least favorite (Figs. 57, 67). The first one of ivory was made in 1909 by Happy Jack. At the insistence of a storekeeper known to the Eskimos as "Kopturok," or "Big Head," he copied a billiken statuette that was the rage at that time in the United States. Since then, thousands, if not millions, have been made in all sizes by the Alaskan carvers.

The billiken has been a part of the carvers' repertoire for so long that most people, including the present carvers, have no idea what it is, or where it came from. Many think it was an aboriginal Eskimo figurine; others, that it was a Nome-invented caricature of an Eskimo. But the fact is that it was invented by Florence Pretz, an art teacher of Kansas City, Missouri, in 1908, who conjured up a vision of "The God of Things as They Ought to Be," a slogan that appeared on some of her statuettes. Through the sheerest luck, I was able to corroborate Kazingnuk's report that the billiken had been copied from a figurine in 1909 when I discovered in a Seattle curio shop an iron coin bank in the shape of a billiken. A search for the patent numbers on the back of the bank indicated that patents had been granted to Miss Pretz on October 6, 1908, for an image called "billiken."

Originally the billiken was carved in ivory only as a figurine, but it is now made also as earrings, bracelet links, necklaces, rings, salt and pepper shakers, letter openers, gavels, and almost anything else that might appear to be suitable.

The first billikens in ivory followed the original in every detail, with the oblique eyes and eyebrows, mouth, nostrils, nipples, and navel emphasized with India ink. The figure had well-defined feet, arms, hands, and ears, and a fat belly. However, changes rapidly occurred as a result of several factors, the most important being the urgency for speed in carving. This caused some characteristics to be minimized and others to be abandoned. Hair is no longer indicated, and the feet and toes have degenerated to nothing but a fringe in front with a vertical cut indicating the separation of the feet. In many cases, the nine notches in the fringe that marked the toes have decreased to four, and sometimes only three. The arms and hands, which had always been made tight to the body, are sometimes barely discernible, and the fingers are only slight indentions in the ivory. The face, except for very large billikens, is made without contours, and with the slanting eyes, the smiling mouth, and the nose indicated only with India ink. The stomach in some cases has been reduced to an emaciated condition.

The carvers rarely make large billikens now because they prefer to use the ivory in more profitable or interesting ways. Neither do they carve the extremely small ones that Happy Jack and his friends made with the aid of a magnifying glass, both because they consume too much time and because they have lost their popularity with collectors who once were willing to pay high prices for them.

Additional changes have taken place in the billiken. The most notable occurred during World War II when soldiers stationed at Marks Field suggested the addition of breasts. Thus the "milliken" was born, leading to the creation of entire families—mama, papa, and children.

Other experiments have been made with the billiken but none so successful as the milliken. One is the rarely seen "billiken in a barrel," a male billiken with movable genitals. Carvers occasionally have attempted to portray billikens in different positions or in action, for example, "Spike" Milligrock's billiken bowing in a Japanese-like posture, which had little success.[3]

Many superstitions have evolved from this good-luck carving. The most popular and misleading one, perpetuated by curio stores, is that it was copied after the large face-statue made by Aneuna on Big Diomede Island. This chocky face, three feet high, three feet wide, and ten inches thick, has no resemblance to a billiken, say the Eskimos. It is very disturbing to the carvers that this statue, which was an integral part of their religion when the first fruits of the season were offered to it, has been compared with an isolated bit of American superstition.

[3]Albert Heinrich, "Some Present-Day Acculturative Innovations in a Nonliterate Society," *American Anthropologist*, LII, No. 2 (1950), 240.

Most curio shops enclose with each billiken a couplet something like the following:

> Just rub his tummy or tickle his toes,
> It will bring you good luck—so the story goes.

Billikens have recently been made by Siberian Eskimos under the guidance of the Siberian Arts and Crafts Board in that area. Antropova illustrates three of them carved in 1945 and lodged in the Museum of Anthropology, Soviet Union Academy of Sciences.[4] It is not surprising that this American phenomenon has cropped up in Siberia since the American Eskimo culture at no time grew separately from its Siberian affiliations. The well-defined and complex Eskimo life of Alaska was only one part of a great sea-conscious culture which, with Siberia and Alaska as its opposite sides, held within its confines the islands of St. Lawrence, King, and the Diomedes, and the rich walrus and whale routes. Until the barring of travel recently between the United States and Siberia, the Eskimos considered the Bering Strait, not as a barrier, but as an aveune of travel between the countries. In all probability an American Eskimo had many Siberian relatives.

During the 1910's and 1920's American Eskimos frequently went to Siberia as deck hands on small boats or to work at trading posts. One of the men, Kazingnuk, who was living at a trading post of East Cape at the time of the Bolshevik Revolution in 1917, carved dozens of cribbage boards and figurines which are probably still masquerading as Siberian Eskimo-carved ivory. Any number of American Eskimos could have shown their Siberian friends how to carve a billiken.

Besides the billiken and cribbage board, two other kinds of ivory carvings are competing for favor now. These are bracelets and bird and animal figurines, neither of which was made extensively until about twenty-five years ago and which have supplanted in great measure the bric-a-brac of the early formative years. For the most part they are esthetically pleasing, and in many cases they are fine works of art.

Neither the carved bracelets nor the exquisite and sophisticated bird figurines of today were made by Happy Jack, although he is supposed to have made plain bracelets put together with string and also figurines of walruses, seals, bears, and eagles. The animal and bird figurines found

[4] V.V. Antropova, "Bone Carving of the Present Day Eskimo and Chukchee," *Akademiia Nauk,* XV (1953), 9.

in almost all archeological periods differ greatly from today's carvings. Those of Okvik and Old Bering Sea are impressionistic and highly decorated while those of the more recent Thule culture are very crude.

Today, the St. Lawrence and King Island carvers are noted particularly for the carving of bird figurines (Figs. 62, 63, 67). The finesse of the very realistic ducks and geese made today is attributed to the interest of Admiral (then Capt.) Edward Darlington Jones of the United States Coast Guard in the 1920's. He showed the carvers pictures of birds, especially, and described the way he wanted them made. Over a period of time he selected only the best carvings, and thus a very high standard was established. The King Islanders and the Eskimos from the mainland copied them at that time, when trips between Nome and St. Lawrence Island were made more frequently than now. Two of the best Nome carvers also lived on St. Lawrence Island in the late twenties, George Washington from 1927 to 1931 and Kazingnuk and his family in 1928.

Bird figurines are sold as assorted sets on St. Lawrence Island but usually as solitary figurines by the King Island carvers. Unless one is well acquainted with an individual carver's work, it is sometimes difficult to distinguish between the bird carvings of the two islands.

The paucity of human figurines today contrasts sharply with the hundreds collected between 1860 and 1890 and now reposing in museums (for examples, see Figs. 34, 39, 40). Earlier archeological sites have also been rich in both ivory and wooden human figures. There is little mystery why so few are made today. They were once used as toys for children, which have been supplanted by American-made dolls, or they were religious figures, which are now outmoded. Almost all precontemporary dolls and figurines, particularly those of ceremonial or religious character, showed the naked body, but, after the missionaries and teachers arrived in Alaska, they convinced the Eskimos that it was "bad" to make them in that manner. The contemporary carvers do make a few figurines of fully clothed Eskimos but complain that customers do not buy them, preferring the animals and birds.

Bracelets were first seriously produced in the 1920's when an unknown Eskimo carver began to make them for a man employed by the Alaska Road Commission. Bracelets tied together with string had not proved very practical, but after elastic thread was suggested the carvers produced dozens of kinds. In fact, with the almost unlimited combinations of links and designs possible, they could easily make thousands without duplication.

Despite the bewildering array of bracelets offered for sale, they can generally be classed into four groups according to the predominant kind of link: (1) plain, (2) carved animal or other figurine, (3) engraved, and (4) inlaid (Figs. 78, 79, 80, 82). A subclassification can be made according to the kind of material used, the most common being old, mammoth, and new ivory. The first two are used only for plain links or contrasting material in inlaid bracelets, but new ivory is both engraved and carved.

Plain bracelets, the links of which can be square, oblong, ovate, or petaloid, are usually interspersed with beads or pieces of baleen or old ivory in various shapes (Fig. 80). Although the carver sometimes makes plain bracelets without beads or contrasting material between the main links, he invariably separates carved or engraved bracelet links in this way.

The circumstances surrounding the making of the first animal bracelet, as it is called by both carvers and retailers, have been forgotten, but early carvers were already making small reclining figures of animals with the heads arbitrarily placed to the right just as they are on the present-day animal bracelet (Figs. 77, 78, 79). This consists of five or six links each with a different animal, usually including a seal, a wolf, a polar bear, a whale, a beluga, and a fox. Although no date has been established for the original bracelet, many were being made in 1938 when a famous innovation, the dog-team bracelet, was evolved by "Spike" Milligrock (Fig. 78). According to Kazingnuk, he and Milligrock had discussed the possibility of making this kind for some time, but Milligrock actually carved the first one.[5]

The dog-team bracelet is made with five links carved from white ivory and representing a dog team: a lead dog, three pairs behind him, and a man sitting in a sled, interpersed with old ivory or baleen. The design was so successful that several Diomede carvers made this their principal kind of carving for a while. The original form has not been retained during the past two decades, however, although the changes have been slight. Individual carvers' interpretations have varied the dogs, the sled, and the driver, and so have customers' complaints. For example,

[5]See also Heinrich, "Some Present-Day Acculturative Innovations in a Nonliterate Society," p. 240.

at first the dogs were boldly carved on the links, but the proud, unfortunate animals often lost their heads by catching on clothing. Although the carvers were still making them in this fashion in 1945, ten years later the dogs had become sleek and streamlined, with the head, neck, and contours of the haunches merely a suggestion of the former angular sculpture. The pruning down of the dog has in some cases left only a hump of ivory bounded on one end by a tail and on the other by a knob for the head. But one of the early characteristics, the direction of the head, continues to the present. All of the dogs, including the lead, turn their heads to the outside edge of the bracelet; none looks straight ahead.

A recent innovation, the watchband, is made from all kinds of bracelets. It is simply a bracelet provided with an opening and fastenings for a watch, which can be attached with a steel pin.

There have been some notable failures among figurine bracelet innovations. One of these, the swan bracelet, originated by Kazingnuk about 1950, was a series of identical low-relief swans in flight as viewed from above. After he had finished the first bracelet, he showed it to a trader who assured him that he would buy a number of them, but it became evident after a few months that they were not popular. Despite the fact that Kazingnuk discontinued making them immediately, there were still a few offered for sale at the original price in Nome curio stores in 1955.

The King Islanders tried another innovation that proved unpopular. This was the addition of a cutout (filigree) reindeer, often made as a brooch, to a plain-link bracelet.[6] One reason for its failure was the inability of present-day customers to see that it looked "Eskimo." Birds, polar bears, walruses, seals, kayaks, oomiaks, and parkas have the stamp of the Eskimo culture on them, but not the reindeer in spite of the fact that in the early part of the twentieth century the Eskimos herded thousands of them, and before that they hunted caribou, a wild reindeer.

A bracelet of flamboyant but short-lived success was originated during World War II by Jack Secco, another Diomede Islander (Fig. 82). The bear-head bracelet, as it was known, was a series of ferocious-looking bas-relief bear heads, usually interspersed with baleen links. The eyes and the nose, which consisted of one big nostril, were inlaid with baleen,

[6]These cutout reindeer look very similar to the filigree work of the Samoyeds illustrated by A.E. Nordenskiöld, *The Voyage of the Vega round Asia and Europe* (New York: Macmillan and Co., 1882), p. 70.

the teeth were sharp and pointed, and the wide-open mouth was painted red and outlined with black. Bold, black whiskers radiated from the nose. It has been said that this particular kind of bear head was copied in 1944 from the insignia of the Alaska Department of the Army,[7] but this is extremely doubtful since these were almost exact duplicates of bear heads that were carved in the 1920's.[8] The majority of Diomede carvers made them, but no King Island men. Now even the Diomede carvers rarely make them, not only because there are fewer soldiers to buy these souvenirs specifically aimed at them, but because the majority of the carvers did not like to make them any more than they did the billiken. More will be said about this in chapter 9.

The double bracelet, one of the latest developments in the figurine bracelet, also seems destined to failure. Two bracelets, usually with totally unrelated subject matter, are fastened together side by side, producing a clumsy and garish effect. The carvers could possibly make a more pleasing object by using narrower bracelets, but this would entail more time spent in carving smaller figures, and it would be more difficult to make the holes through which the rubber thread passes.

The engraved or "etched" bracelet, according to the Nome Eskimos, was first made by Shishmaref carvers, who also, before their recent immigration to Nome, made more of these bracelets than any other group (Fig. 78). The first bracelet links of this kind were engraved with unrelated figures or scenes such as a sod igloo, a dog sled, and a walrus. The story bracelet, which relates a simple tale in six scenes, was developed only a few years ago. However, narratives akin to this were occasionally engraved on slabs of ivory in the later phases of the old-style engraving about the time of the first European contact in northern Alaska, early in the nineteenth century. A carver of this kind of bracelet usually has only one or two stories to relate and makes numerous bracelets with identical story and scenes. Tingook engraved the same story and scenes on every one of his bracelets of 1954 and 1955. Diomede Island carvers also make engraved bracelets now although animal bracelets always have been their specialty.

The carver uses the same scenes not only because he wishes to save

[7]Heinrich, "Some Present-Day Acculturative Innovations in a Nonliterate Society," p. 240.

[8]A carved tusk with similar bear heads, collected about 1927, is in the collection of Mrs. A. Hotovitsky (Fig. 75), and two tusks of the same character in the United States National Museum, Nos. 332296 and 332297, were collected by Aleš Hrdlička in 1926.

time in carving but because he believes that constant practice produces perfection. One of the carvers said that, if a new story were carved on each bracelet, it would "look like a beginner's." This rationalization is partially true, for, if the carver were to engrave out a story for the first time with the haste that he usually employs, the initial results would be considered inferior work by him and the other carvers.

Inlaid bracelets are of two kinds. Both are constructed of a white link, one with a paper-thin oval, square, or rectangular piece of ivory or baleen glued into a very shallow depression on the top of it, and the other with pieces of dark ivory or baleen inserted into it to form various geometric patterns.

The first inlaid bracelet of the first type is supposed to have been made about 1937 by Kazingnuk and a friend of his at the suggestion of a man employed in Nome. The inlaid bracelet of the second type probably originated at Teller. By 1946 both kinds were being made on Little Diomede Island,[9] but the carvers there evidently were not convinced until 1948 that they were marketable items. This seems strange in view of the fact that numerous bracelets were sold in Nome during the war years from 1942 to 1946. George Washington, who makes some of the best inlaid bracelets, could not keep up with his orders at that time.

The making of inlaid bracelets is tedious and exacting work, and carvers who can cut inlaid pieces with the necessary precision receive the praise of others. George Washington's first bracelets were made of thicker links than his present ones, which are thin and waferlike, in order to conserve ivory and because of the customers' desire for a more delicate bracelet.

There have been few innovators in contemporary carving; most of the carvers have preferred to stay within the comfortable confines of tradition. The difference between the innovator and the versatile carver is the addition of an adventuresome spirit. The former will try something from his own imagination with no definite assurance of a sale, as well as from someone else's suggestion. In his moments of adventure he casts away the extreme premium put on time and money and launches on his risky journey. The brave spirits who have appeared seem to have created enough objects for others to copy for some time. Happy Jack was one of the greatest. Contemporary carvers who have carved a number of origi-

[9]Heinrich, "Some Present-Day Acculturative Innovations in a Nonliterate Society," p. 241.

nal objects are Pikongonna of King Island, Milligrock of Diomede Island, and Kazingnuk of Diomede Island and Nome.

Milligrock, who carved the first dog-team bracelet, has tried many other things as well. Kazingnuk is willing to try anything that anyone may suggest and has several inventions of his own including the ill-fated swan bracelet. In 1928 he made cribbage boards with many complete animals in low relief, "like a totem pole." Although the designs on it were his own imagination, the idea of carving it was suggested to him by a trader who furnished the ivory and paid him for the work.

His latest innovation is a dove on a pedestal, a product entirely of his own imagination. After finishing several, he took them to a merchant who asked, "What is it? A ptarmigan?"

"No," he replied, "It's a dove."

"A dove?" questioned the trader. "Why do you make a dove?"

"It means peace. Every home should have one, and when people fight they look at it, and everything is good again."

Kazingnuk said that he had nourished the idea for many years, ever since Happy Jack had taught him how to make an eagle with its wings outspread, clutching a ball or a reindeer in its talons.

Erotic elements, which are seen occasionally, are concomitant with the coming of white culture to the Eskimo area. Early historic Eskimo figurines occasionally carried a suggestion of exaggerated sexual characteristics, but the ancient Eskimo cultures of Okvik and Old Bering Sea reveal nothing of this kind, not even rudiments of a fertility cult.[10]

Hoffman points out that among all the examples of graphic art of the nineteenth-century Eskimo he found only one instance that he could consider a sexual symbol: "The peculiar marking up on the top of the head, which no doubt is intended to represent wrinkles or folds of the skin, is also the rude symbol of the female genitals as drawn by the Eskimo, and of which one single instance is found in the collections of the National Museum, and is reproduced in figure 28."[11] Even this

[10]The so-called "Okvik Madonna" may be a fertility figure since a small area in the front of the figurine has been interpreted as a representation of the female organs, but this is not conclusive.

[11]Walter James Hoffman, *The Graphic Art of the Eskimos* (U.S. National Museum, Annual Report for 1895, Washington, D.C., 1897), p. 841. Only three archeological pieces that might be sexual symbols have come to my attention. See Henry B. Collins, Jr., *Prehistoric Art of the Alaskan Eskimo* (Smithsonian Miscellaneous Collections, Vol. LXXXI, No. 4, 1929), Pl. 16; Therkel Mathiassen, "Ancient Eskimo Settlements in the Kangamiut Area," *Meddelelser om Grønland*, XCI (1931), 1-150, Fig. 35; Pl. 5, No. 9.

identification is doubtful since many of the "symbols" which were drawn for Hoffman (and which he considered incipient writing) were done by highly acculturated men, mainly Aleuts.

Only when the bearers of a foreign culture suggested it have the carvers made graphic or sculptural representations of eroticism. At some time during the past few decades visitors to Nome induced some of the carvers to make two erotic sculptures that continue their furtive existence today: the previously mentioned billiken in a barrel with movable male genitals, and the "six-legged bear," which represents two copulating bears. Several of the latter were produced toward the end of the summer of 1955 by a carver who had been commissioned by a saloonkeeper.

During the same year the King Island carvers were selling *oosuks,* or walrus penis bones, for the first time, something that afforded them no end of amusement. They shrugged their shoulders, saying, "We don't know why anyone wanted that old piece of bone, but if they want to pay ten dollars for it, it's all right with us." The demand for these had begun only a few seasons before on St. Lawrence Island where soldiers suggested to the carvers that they attach carved animal heads to both ends of a well-polished bone. The result was called a "conversation piece" by those who took them home.

Only very few of the men willingly carve these erotic pieces, and then they do it secretly. They have learned that the white man is enigmatically reticent about the most natural things in the world, but at the same time willing to talk about things that should not be talked about. The carver is at a loss to understand why men want to have such objects, but he gladly takes the unusually high price and ceases trying to understand.

EIGHT: The Artist's Standards

EVERY Eskimo man of the islands is an ivory carver, but not even the best carver is considered an artist, nor would any Eskimo admit that he himself is an artist except for those few who, in media other than ivory, have capitalized on their own talent and the Eskimos' artistic reputation. To the Eskimo carver an artist is a man who paints and draws in a world outside the carver's own knowledge and environment. There is no concept of artist in his way of thinking—his beautiful creations have resulted from a necessary, though enjoyable, occupation, not from an esoteric pursuit. Despite the fact that the non-Eskimo world might assess a carver and his work as artist and art, he will say, not in negation, but as a statement of fact, "I'm no artist." His inability to view himself as a creative artist does not, however, subtract from the real artistry of the best pieces.

Undoubtedly the carvers who are classed as "expert" by their fellow carvers are the ones who can be called "artists" in our judgment. Probably the most satisfactory term of classification for the average carver is "artist-craftsman," for he is sometimes one and sometimes the other. His sculpture is truly the work of an artist for he is constantly reinterpreting his subject matter. When he begins to make a bear he can have a dozen alternative lines of attack within the generalized form in his mind. He is also an artist when developing his ideas in engraving. Very little of his work is completely repetitious or stylized patterns. But his work comes closer to being a craft when he makes certain stereo-

132

typed objects such as bracelets, beads, billikens, and copies of foreign souvenir gadgets. He is sometimes both artist and craftsman. For example, the animal bracelet or necklace is often an exciting piece of jewelry, the remarkable poses of the minute animals reflecting a multiplicity of invention and interpretation (Figs. 77, 78, 79). Once in a great while, moreover, there is a carver who is completely an artist, who is bored and impatient with the copying and repetition that are so often the lot of the average carver. Even when he makes many objects seemingly alike, each one is freshly interpreted and alive with the spontaneity of creation.

As might be expected in a culture where carving is as common as eating and has been used for purposes other than pure enjoyment, or gratification of the senses, the criteria by which the excellence of a carver is judged differ greatly from those that would be used in another culture. These criteria reflect the carvers' attitude not only toward their work as art, but toward their whole way of life. Some of their bases of judging a carver are the same as those used in other areas of their workaday life, but a man who is rated low as a carver would not necessarily be rated the same in any other work.

The carvers will discuss freely the characteristics a carver should have to be good, but they are unwilling to discuss the merits of any individual carver. They will gladly supply the names of all the carvers who in their opinions are "expert," but they will not utter the names of those who are not. This reveals, more clearly than a discussion of each individual's merits, the repute in which he is held as an artist. An Eskimo carver asked his opinion of another who is not considered "expert" will answer evasively, with apologetic qualifications, "Oh, he can't carve everything," or, "He is getting old," or, "He has not had much practice." He will not give his direct opinion or discuss the other in any way.

Each carver knows his own rank in the scale of competence, and so do all the other carvers. Although the criteria the carvers themselves hold important are many and rigorous, over half of the island carvers are termed expert by the others. For those who have been reared in a culture where artists, no matter how good, are in the minority, it is difficult to comprehend one in which the total male population is composed of "artists," and furthermore where 50 per cent of them are considered best by their own standards. For instance, of the twenty-one males over twenty-one years of age on Little Diomede Island, eleven are considered expert, fulfilling all requirements.

Probably the most important criterion by which excellence is judged is the ability to make everything. This versatility encompasses both carving in the round and engraving, and the making of both new or foreign objects and those which have long been a traditional part of the carving industry. Individual Eskimo carvers have been put to this test many times, and few have been known to fail it. Pikongonna was once asked to copy the "Last Supper" of Leonardo da Vinci on a small piece of ivory.

"It was the hardest thing I ever did," he said, "but when I finished I liked it better than anything I ever carved."

Versatility, which always stands as the prime consideration in judging another carver, includes the most creative and satisfying of all acts to the carvers, the making of figurines. Thus, a carver who in their opinion is a well-rounded carver, and who can do anything with a piece of ivory, is a man who would be called an artist by our standards. His complete knowledge of his material and proficiency in its creative use overshadow the technical problems of his medium. Although his plans might sometimes be altered because of the waywardness of the ivory, he is able to extemporize satisfactorily even though the result is not that of his preconceived mental image. A lifetime of mastering his medium has not dulled the creativeness of the Eskimo artist of figurines. On the contrary, the problems and catastrophes that appear now and then only make him more determined to meet them head on, and so, while a dozen tusks may suit his every purpose and tease him into a false security, he knows that the thirteenth may be the one to challenge his sleeping ingenuity.

The ability to copy, developed to a remarkable degree by the Eskimo carvers, has undoubtedly contributed to their versatility. Not only are they able to construct a two-dimensional picture from the three-dimensional world, but with equal ease they can carve in three dimensions from a two-dimensional representation. This ability is not a recent one aided by academic education, for none of the early carvers had difficulty in interpreting unfamiliar objects seen for the first time in a photograph or illustration. Not only were they able to identify familiar objects in a completely foreign medium—a book or a magazine—but from the beginning they were able to carve even unfamiliar ones in three dimensions, adding depth that a picture never reveals.

Beechey, in 1826, showed Eskimos of Kotzebue Sound plates of animals in *Rees's Cyclopaedia.* He reports that "the Esquimaux are very superior in this respect to the South Sea Islanders and immediately recognized every animal they were acquainted with...."[1]

This ability, which we take for granted in our everyday life, acquainted as we are with the printed page, is not characteristic of all primitive peoples. Reports have been made of the singular ineptness of some in identifying even familiar objects from a photograph. For example, Jochelson says of some of the northern Siberian tribes:

> To what extent the artistic instinct is developed among the Koryak may be judged from the fact that they easily recognized drawings and pictures in the books which I showed them, and always recognized the photographs of their friends. On the contrary, the northern Yakut, the Tungus, and even the Yukaghir, frequently failed to recognize photographs which I took of their friends. Some of them failed to recognize that the photographs represented human faces.[2]

Straight copying of a two-dimensional illustration was no problem at all to the early carvers. Happy Jack, in particular, was famous for his ability to copy illustrations from magazines and newspapers exactly even to the shadings of a halftone. A portrait of Theodore Roosevelt, a man panning gold from a stream, and a group of men standing in front of a store were so much like the illustrations from which he copied that they appeared to be printed on the ivory. One of his most unusual pieces is a facsimile of a Packer's Tar Soap wrapper which is now in the whaling museum at Mystic Seaport, Connecticut (Fig. 53). Little is known about the history of this piece, but it is presumed to have been sent to the factory by some friend or representative of the company after he had commissioned Happy Jack to make it.

The Alaskan Eskimo carvers' pride and competence in copying are among the characteristics that differentiate them from the central Canadian Eskimo carvers whose contemporary art was first stimulated by the Canadian Handicrafts Guild in 1949, fifty years after the contemporary art of Alaska had begun. Entirely different in concept, material, and

[1] F.W. Beechey, *Narrative of a Voyage to the Pacific and Beering's Strait, 1825-1828* (London, 1831), Part I, p. 298.

[2] Vladimir Ilich Jochelson, *The Koryak* (Memoirs of the American Museum of Natural History, Vol. X, 1905-6), p. 658.

motifs from the art of the Alaskan Eskimo, it had none of the rich artistic heritage of the Bering Sea Eskimo upon which to draw. The Canadian Eskimo had done little ornamentation or sculpture within the memory of the first explorers and traders of the nineteenth century, and there is little archeological art in the region. Despite this barren background, they have developed a very forceful stone sculpture under the tutelage of the guild.

According to James Houston, who is closely allied with this work, "The carver is usually reluctant to copy or repeat a subject of his own, or indeed anybody else's work."[3] Whether this is a peculiarity of the Canadian Eskimo's outlook on his new art, or whether it is the influence of the guild, is hard to ascertain from the printed sources, but neither the prehistoric nor the modern Alaskan Eskimos have been reluctant to copy or repeat a subject.

In fact, copying is one of the traits of both modern and archeological Alaskan Eskimo art. Today the carver makes hundreds of objects alike for ultimate non-Eskimo consumption. This is true of the southwest Eskimos, also, for they both paint dishes and spoons with the same designs and make masks with identical parts.

Archeological finds of all periods reveal that duplication and repetition have not been confined to the present. The stylized bird motif of the Old Bering Sea Eskimo was reused time after time, not only on harpoon heads and harpoon foreshafts but on many unidentified objects. Many Punuk harpoon heads are so much alike that they are indistinguishable one from the other. Identical Thule birds and dolls were turned out by the dozens, and the small figurines used as drag handles by the nineteenth-century Alaskan Eskimos were duplicated over and over, as were the arrangements of designs on needlecases and bag handles.

Engraved bracelets made by Shishmaref carvers are rarely surpassed by any other Eskimos, but the carvers who make only these bracelets are not considered expert either by other carvers or by themselves. One told me, "I'm not good. I can make only those bracelets." According to the customers he ranks as a superior artist. He could probably carve other objects exceedingly well if he tried, but since he is very successful with these bracelets he has little time for anything else.

[3]Department of Northern Affairs and National Resources, Canada, *Canadian Eskimo Art* (Ottawa, 1957), p. 27.

Next in importance to versatility is the ability to make animals and birds as realistic as possible, or "just like life." However, in spite of the fact that the carvers constantly criticize carved animals' facial expressions, physical stances, and bodily proportions that are not accurate, their final interpretation of realism is an idealistic one that never reaches the faithful reproduction to which they aspire. Their concept of realism will be treated at length in another chapter.

These two requirements, versatility and the ability to protray animals realistically, are the most difficult to fulfill, and a carver who unquestionably possesses the remaining qualifications of an expert carver will never be considered a top-ranking performer without them. The following characteristics, all related to manual dexterity, are also considered of great importance by the carvers: (1) neatness and precision in both engraving and carving, (2) ability to work swiftly, (3) ability to obtain a high polish, and (4) proficiency in applying color to incisions.

Precision in the carver's work is closely related to the ability to copy and finds its highest expression in accurate visual measurements, which every carver is able to make. Spatial relationships are easily transferred to concrete measurements by all adult Eskimos including the women, who rarely use any measuring device in the sewing of fur garments.

This ability is not confined to carving and sewing but is inextricably interwoven with the Eskimo's whole life. For the main part, the environment of the Bering Strait Eskimo is a monotonous stretch of land in which there are few of the obvious landmarks of a more rugged locale. Acute observation is essential in order to find one's way amidst the monotony of this land and sea. The Eskimo has been trained from childhood to gauge the distances of his natural environment, a very difficult feat in the gray dusk of a winter day when the white of the snow reflects the deep grayness of the sky, often leaving the ground contourless and the sky merely an extension of the earth. Objects at a distance take on meaningless relationships to the untrained eye—in one instant a quixotic mirage of great distance, and, in another, one of extreme proximity.

Under these difficult conditions an Eskimo must develop judgment and accuracy that can mean life or death—in a jump across the water from jagged ice, throwing a spear at a polar bear, or driving a sled over treacherous terrain. The young boy begins his training when he goes seal hunting with his father at ten or twelve years of age after a period of learning at home with his toy bows and arrows and harpoons. Memory work as well as alertness is emphasized. The children are trained to remember a landmark or distinctive object after observing it only once. The whole of an object is observed first, the details fitted in after that.

The present-day Alaskan carvers make their hundreds of figurines and engravings of their own environment almost completely from memory.[4] They almost never carve or engrave with a model before them. Occasionally, they may reinforce their recollection of specific postures of animals by studying real-life photographs, but they never copy directly from them. They teach the children with no model other than memory or possibly another carving.

The carvers today easily transfer measurements to the English system of inches, feet, yards, and miles. The Eskimo man estimates yards and miles as accurately in his hunting as he does inches in his carving. When I was photographing activities of the ivory carvers, I discovered that I did not need a range finder as long as I had one in the form of an ivory carver, who without fail could visualize the exact distance from an object to the lens of the camera.

The fine degree to which visual estimation is carried was exemplified once when I ordered an ivory ring from a carver. After I had shown him the finger on which I intended to wear it, nothing more was said. I therefore assumed that the measuring would come later when he found time to make the ring. But after only a few days' time he gave me the completed ring in the exact size. When I asked him how he had arrived at the size without measuring, he replied that my finger had looked about the same size as his wife's! Even more surprisingly, I later discovered that it was actually another carver, with a supply of sperm whale tooth ivory, who had made the ring. It had not changed size in being transferred to a carver whom I had never met.

One of the carvers told me simply that he carried his measurements "in the brain," and that he had to look only once to know a dimension. An ability akin to this is also demonstrated in the making of unstable-appearing figurines which stand, nevertheless, with perfect aplomb. They are made without being tested for the center of gravity at any time during the carving. Jochelson has reported the similar skill of the Koryak

---

[4]Hans Himmelheber (*Eskimokünstler* [Stuttgart: Strecker and Schröder, 1938], p. 164) found that this was true also of the painting of the southwest Alaskan Eskimo.

in accurately placing the center of gravity of even the most complicated figures such as men in different positions playing a drum or dancing.[5]

Once the techniques of carving and engraving have been mastered, it is almost as simple as breathing for the very best carvers to create a realistic bear from a resilient block of ivory. This is not what the carvers call difficult, but rather the monotonous operations of scraping file marks, sandpapering, applying the final gloss, putting in color, and even the simple tasks of cutting out plain bracelets or making billikens that conform to a rigid style. For the young and inexperienced carver, however, figurines and engraving are legitimately "hard" to do. The carvers believe that they need many years of practice to become proficient, and only the proficient are able to carve with great speed. Speed is recognized not only for the skill involved in carving swiftly, but for the equally important consideration that the carver, by working fast, will have a better income than if he carved slowly.

The development of speed by the best carvers has led to various kinds of conventionalizations that have decreased the realism of their portrayals more than they realize. Although most of these are subtle and subject to various interpretations, the outstanding one is the use of the zigzag to indicate feathers on birds and for various kinds of fill-ins and accentuation of lineal motifs. The method of making the zigzag has already been described in chapter 5. Some of the carvers say that they would like to make "real" feathers but that the amount of time it would take to make them would be prohibitive, probably four or five times as much as it takes for the quick rocking of the flat end of the graver. To the majority of carvers, the zigzag makes "pretty good-looking" feathers.

The method of indicating density has changed from era to era. Before prolonged European contact, but still in the nineteenth century, density was usually shown by crosshatched or parallel slashes in the ivory (for example, see Figs. 45, 46). During the early experimental period of contemporary carving it was often achieved by innumerable dots as in newspaper halftones. This tedious pricking of the ivory with a needle was soon discontinued in favor of the time-saving zigzag.

The need for speed has led also to the conventionalization of placing the heads of reclining animals facing in one direction in both figurine bracelets and sculptured animals of that type. The majority are carved

[5] Jochelson, *The Koryak*, Figs. 169, a-e; 172, a; and 170, a and b.

with the head facing the animal's right when it is lying down (Figs. 77-79). Happy Jack is supposed to have originated the tradition of placing the animals' heads in that direction, and some of the carvers, believing an immovable law governs that position, say it is "wrong" to turn them to the left. Actually, whichever way a carver does adopt is time-saving, for once he has established the practice of making animals turning in one direction, he can work more swiftly.

The best carvers have developed the practice of carving several like objects one after another. For instance, one may carve three or four reclining animals and then four standing bears, or another may carve several bears and then a series of letter openers. Some carvers make dozens of billikens in a row. The slower carvers usually diversify their carving by making only one of a kind before beginning another. But no matter what sequence they use, once they have begun an object they work on it until it is finished.

Some carvers have developed themes that they use over and over in their carving. For example, Oarlaranna in the past few years has used the motif of a bird on a cactuslike tree for dozens of paper knives. A man may engrave the same design many times on cribbage boards, brooches, or bracelets.

"If they would do a different one each time," Kazingnuk said, "it would take too much time to think each new one out."

This is again opposite to the approach of the central Canadian Eskimo. One of the Canadian carvers, Kopekoolik, was asked to carve a walrus similar to one he had just finished. His answer was, "You see that I can carve the likeness of a walrus! Why would you want another one?"

The explanation given was this: "He had proven himself a carver of walrus, and that was enough. But when the idea of carving a caribou was suggested to him, he immediately became excited. He had yet to prove himself a carver of caribou. And he went to find some stone."[6] Nevertheless, a number of objects for sale recently by these Eskimos reveal numerous duplications by the same carver.

Some of the slower carvers who are thought of as very good would be considered even better if they could work faster. The combination of excellence and slowness in carving is directly related to age, for when carvers reach the sixties and seventies they slow down their production

[6]*Canadian Eskimo Art,* p. 33.

but retain their excellence. Sometimes, when an old man's carving is considerably inferior to the best, it is said that this is so because "he is an old man." This is a deliberate rationalization and often an excuse for a carver who never was very good. If a man was a good carver when he was in his prime, he will be a good carver when he is old, and there are many old carvers to substantiate this opinion. Usually, if an expert carver's eyesight fails, or he is unable to expend the energy needed to finish an object properly, he will stop carving. Once a man has produced top-grade goods, there is little that will induce him to make inferior ones.

A few carvers insist that they do not engrave because their eyesight is poor. However, although it is true that extremely fine engraving puts a strain on the eyes, this reason is used mainly as an excuse for not engraving. Andrew Tingook, who is ranked as the best engraver in Nome today, is an unusual man who, though threatened with blindness, nevertheless engraves very small figures on bracelet links with the aid of a magnifying glass.

Polishing is arduous and tedious work, as are the scraping and filing preparatory for the final polishing. The carvers consider these the "hardest to do," and all dislike the tasks. A smooth finish and a high gloss reflect a tremendous amount of work by the carver, and they are often commented upon by other carvers. Indeed, an ideal of the Eskimo, the industrious man, is embodied in this part of the carving activity. Laziness would be disastrous for the carver at the two extremes of his carving, either as a hunter getting the raw material for his carving or in the final preparation of his product for the market. Without a fine gloss, he could not sell it either to the transient public or to clearing houses such as the Alaska Native Arts and Crafts Clearing House.

The carver does not at any time during the making of an object test the progress of the smoothing by feeling it with his hand. Even the casting away of ivory dust is accomplished by blowing or wiping with a rag or, at the most, a swift brush of his fingers. He will hold the piece and look at it many times from different angles during the finishing of it, testing the smoothness with his eyes. Even when he decides that it is ready to sell he will not rub his hand over it to feel its exquisite surface.

The successful application of color into incised ivory is also a tiresome duty, and one related more to perseverance in rubbing than to dexterity with a graver. Depth of incision has no bearing on how permanently the color will stay, for those who are most competent in this respect can put richly dark, permanent color into any mark. The secret is successive and opulent application of the color, whether it is powdered graphite, cigarette ash, or India ink. It is rubbed vigorously until the carver is assured that it will not rub off or "fade."

Strangely enough, originality is not considered important enough to use as a measure of a carver's excellence. Originality is of prime consideration only when an innovation becomes a successful item in the carver's repertoire, as discussed in the preceding chapter. Because the monetary returns from carvings are so small at best, the carver feels that to take time away from the regular carving for experimentation is too great a gamble. But, once a carver has taken the step toward an original idea, he usually continues with it until it has proven its worth or has become another failure. Often an incentive for producing something new is given to a carver by some outside person, and when that happens he is less reluctant to depart from his usual carvings. The idea for a new kind of object does not, however, always originate from outside the carver, although it is true that many of the forms and kinds of objects carved during this period of contemporary carving have been either suggested or approved by the buying public. The styles and motifs used, even when influenced by outside suggestions, have been taken from the Eskimo carver's own heritage and imagination.

NINE: The Artist's Concept of Realism

T HE carvers are convinced that their figurines are completely realistic, and their most frequent and severe criticism stems from the lack of realism in certain carvings. They are preoccupied constantly with making their sculpture, particularly of animals, "more lifelike," but this realism when examined closely is superficial and idealized, and, in spite of the carvers' compulsive endeavors to mirror every detail exactly, their interpretations often fall far short.

The carvers contemplate their subjects with the boldness of an artist rather than the narrowness of a copyist. They are concerned only with the impression that results from merely a glance, an impression like that received by an experienced hunter who differentiates between a white and a red fox on a hillside with only a fleeting look. Thus, in spite of the insistence on the importance of making the carving "lifelike," it is not a photographic copy that is finally achieved, but a distinctive figure given recognizable form through the artistry of several realistic strokes. Much of this effect is achieved through the judicious use of characteristic postures and attitudes and diagnostic features of the animals.

The Bering Strait carver's art is much more realistic, however, than the symbolic art of the southwest Alaskan Eskimo or the recent sculpture of the Canadian Eskimo. The recent government-fostered stone carving in Canada is conceptually more closely related to both Koryak carvings and a collection of wooden figures from St. Lawrence Island than those of the Bering Strait (Fig. 89). All of those carvings—Canadian Eskimo,

Koryak, St. Lawrence Island—contain a suggestion of distortion or the grotesque, both of which the contemporary Alaskan carvers avoid. In fact, the Bering Strait carvers would consider that kind of carving as the mark of a beginner not yet in command of his ideas and tools. Carvings of this kind puzzle them. One of the Diomede carvers, upon being shown illustrations of the Canadian objects, exclaimed, "What's the matter with them? Don't they know how to make things?"

The question arises whether or not the billiken is a distortion with its eternally smiling mouth, exaggerated Oriental features, unnatural arms, and even more unnaturally shortened legs. The billiken is a distortion when viewed as a deviation from a human being, but to the Eskimo carver of the present it is only a faithful copy of a little figure made fifty years ago. It is not a distortion of the carver's natural world, but a correct copy of a foreign object brought into his culture. This fact probably explains why so many of the carvers willingly carve a figure that, viewed objectively, is actually a caricatural conception of their own physical features.

Selected diagnostic characteristics of animals are of primary concern to the contemporary carvers. It is a rare man who makes just a fox or a bear; he makes a red fox or a white fox, a polar bear or a brown bear. The carvers differentiate the white fox from the red fox, for example, by making the legs of the former shorter, and they indicate the differences between the polar bear and the brown bear by the smaller size of the brown bear's palms and the greater amount of fur on the polar bear's front legs.

The many birds they make are also carefully delineated with regard to the features that distinguish them in real life. For example, they make the Canada goose with greater thickness than any other birds, marking its magnificent wings boldly with graphite or ink on the pure white ivory (Fig. 67). They portray the eider duck in all of its delicacy, emphasizing the topknotted head (Fig. 62). One of the men, Kazingnuk, who makes doves, said that he never represents the feathers of this bird because "those birds never show their feathers." The carvers are very careful to distinguish between the winter and summer plumage of snowbirds and ptarmigans (Fig. 63). The birds in winter dress are almost perfectly white, with only the tips of the feathers, the eyes, the bill, and the feet colored.

Occasionally the carvers indicate an outstanding characteristic of a bird or animal that is not obvious when the figurine is displayed in its normal position on a table. An example of this is a hollow space under the front flippers of a walrus, just as it is found in the living animal at rest. This can be seen only when the carving is examined from below. It is evident that early-day objects were made to be looked at from all angles, but today's objects are usually placed on a flat surface for display. Even at that, hidden areas are still remembered in the carvings to complete the feeling of a whole animal. Sometimes a carver will polish the underside, which will never show.

Some of the carvers make rolling folds of skin on the back of the walrus' neck. A man who carves this bit of realism is commended by his fellow carvers, for they know that this takes a great deal of time, but even many who would like to do the same in their faithfulness to realism nevertheless make the neck smooth in their haste.

The need to hurry is often bemoaned. One of the King Island carvers told me, "They don't carve much like that nowadays. There were a couple of fellows long ago, carve bear heads. They could carve every bit of it, eyes, teeth, just like real. They just can't duplicate it today. They just don't have the time to do it now, even with all the tools the white men brought."

The best carvers, however, do not depend on small characteristic features only to carry out realism, but attain it also through motion and fluidity in their carvings. The most poorly carved animals lack not only specific physical characteristics but gracefulness as well, and often the unrealistic qualities of the best carvings are obscured by the moving and interpretive grace given to them by the carver.

"Stiff carvings" usually are attributed to "boys" by the older carver, a designation which means that they do not have the indication of maturity which carvings by experienced men are supposed to have. Care in representing physical characteristics is taught the boy from the very first, but fluent style comes through practice and talent.

Most of Pikongonna's bears, of which he is a master, represent flexible, mobile animals—walking, scenting danger, or merely relaxing. He often criticizes himself for having sold a bear whose nose was too short or front legs too thin. Constantly trying to achieve what he thinks is perfection, he says, "I try harder all the time to make it better and more like in real life."

Superior carvers, such as Pikongonna, differentiate between animals not only by easily recognized characteristics but by more subtle observations. For example, the brown bear is more limber than the polar bear, and its hind legs stretch out more when it is in a relaxed position.

In walruses a relaxed attitude is indicated by having the hind flippers falling flat on the table. Kazingnuk, however, likes to make some of his walruses in an attitude of tenseness, with the back flippers "in the shape of a pup tent, maybe like it is waiting for something." Even the seals, the easiest and simplest of the animals to carve, must come up to certain standards. For example, one of the carvers stated that "seals must not look straight ahead because they don't do that much."

Temporary conditions of birds are noted, also. For instance, one of Sanmarana's snow geese had a very short neck, which he explained as being "all hunched up. He's cold." An unknown carver once made an eider duck with its head close to its right wing, the left one raised high. This meant, one of the carvers said, that the duck was trying to get warm.

Pikongonna always carves snowbirds with the bill open, revealing a dusky red interior (Fig. 63). "We like to do it that way because they are always singing," he said.

Although Pikongonna is one of the most competent carvers today, and one of the most faithful devotees of realism, he sacrifices many things for practicality. For example, his walking bears, of which he has made hundreds, do not have a natural stance. All four feet of the bear are made flush to the undersurface. If he made them physically accurate one or two of the legs would be lifted off the ground to show progression in walking. He substituted balance for realism in this case for he felt that it would be difficult to achieve the former with only two of the four legs.

Two conventionalizations, the bear's head and the zigzag, which have already been discussed, have little relationship to realism (Fig. 82). The wide-open bear's mouth flanked by whiskers to represent ferocity has come in for the most adverse criticism lately. The feature that most sorely distresses the critics is the whiskers, which bears do not possess.

One carver asked, "Bears don't have whiskers, so why should they put whiskers like that on a bear?" The use of them is contrary to the general feeling about realism, but some of the carvers feel that their inclusion adds immeasurably to the fierceness of the animal. No carver can give an adequate explanation of why they were first used. One man said, "I think they look more fierce that way, but they still don't look right." Probably the original purpose was to create balance between the top of the face and the bottom, which was heavy with the expansive mouth.

It is of interest to point out that a carving in stone called "Angry Bear" by Sarkee, a Cape Dorset (Canada) carver, is made with whiskers radiating from the upper part of his face.[1]

The carvers differentiate birds not only by size, but by the use of the zigzag in different widths and positions on the birds to indicate wing size and the general texture of feathers. A few of the carvers who remember the very realistically drawn feathers Happy Jack made on the eagle think that the zigzag is a very poor substitute for feathers, but they accept it as a time-saving solution as well as because of its firm adoption by the majority of carvers. To some of them, this appears to be the "only way" that feathers should be carved, and, when feathers are incised in a more realistic way with scallops and striations to indicate single plumes, they say they "look funny." The zigzag for the representation of feathers has become so common that the carvers view the actual differences between birds through this conventionalization.

Another conventionalization aimed toward preserving lifelike characteristics is the placement of three dots on either side of a seal's face to represent whiskers. Although supposedly mirroring a natural feature, a most unrealistic motif—three bulletlike holes—is used. Not only that, but the holes are too large in proportion to the size of the seal. Carvers often say that they "don't look right," but they cannot offer any alternatives. They feel that they should not omit the whiskers because they are as important in portraying a seal as tusks in a walrus.

The desire for speed in all aspects of their carving has led the carvers to dispense with many realistic characteristics such as texture of hair or fur. The carvers say that it would take from three to four times as long

---

[1]Department of Northern Affairs and National Resources, Canada, *Canadian Eskimo Art* (Ottawa, 1957), p. 17.

to make fur as it actually looks on a polar bear or a fox. When Happy Jack first made the popular fox-head umbrella handles of the early twentieth century, no one would have bought them if they had been made with a smooth surface. But now the carvers' reluctance to create shaggy-furred beasts is reinforced by the Alaska Native Arts and Crafts Clearing House, which desires pieces that are highly polished, smooth, and easily cleaned.

Another reason for the carvers' departure from their ideal of realism is their concept of the value of ivory, which we have discussed above. Unconsciously torn between their devotion to realism and their equal devotion to keeping ivory a semiprecious substance, they rarely cover their carved figures excessively with design or color. The walrus, which is a dark brown animal, is always kept white. The seal is made white, in spite of its variegated aspects, and a brown or black bear is rarely colored or made of darker ivory. Even the birds, which are given wings and feathers of colored incisions, are actually only highlighted, for the breasts, necks, and legs are left free of color. Rarely is any color but black used on a piece of sculpture. The Eskimo carver feels that the ivory is as important as the figure, and that black is more dramatic in contrast than any other color could be.

Human figures, of all figurines made, are least lifelike. They are usually immobile, inactive, standing figures looking straight ahead. The faces have no life, and the features are often only several gashes filled with graphite. It is an anomaly that, while some carvers take great pains with animal mouths and eyes, inserting ivory or baleen inlays, the highlights of the human face are minimized or neglected altogether. Little action is portrayed, either obvious or implied. Exceptions to this are made by a limited number of carvers who have experimented with bulkily clothed figures fishing, spearing a bear, chasing ducks, and the like. Beyond that, there is little to suggest a dynamic, living creature.

When an observer speaks of a figure as reflecting certain human reactions, he is usually speaking from his own cultural point of view. It is possible that earlier Eskimo figurines did reflect such reactions in some stereotyped or conventionalized manner of which we are unaware. The contemporary carvers themselves attribute the emptiness and stiffness of their human beings to the lack of practice, an explanation used for all kinds of inadequate work, no matter what the real reason may be.

The head and face have been emphasized more than the body in all archeological and ethnological periods. But, although eyebrows were often carefully incised; eyes were meticulously inlaid with ivory or baleen; and ears, tattoo marks, and labrets were indicated, inner emotions never penetrated the façade. Human figures made by the ancient Bering Strait Eskimos are generally noted, on the one hand, for the realistic highlights of the figure but, on the other, for the lack of fluidity and over-all movement. With but few exceptions, neither the body nor the face suggests action or emotion. The body is a straight piece, indicative only of being, not living, and often legs and arms are omitted.

The same applies to figurines of the four periods in which the greatest number of human figures were made: Okvik, Thule, late prehistoric, and early prehistoric. Many Okvik figurines are blocks of ivory with no arms or legs, topped with a head (Figs. 8-12). The bodies were sometimes made with a suggestion, here and there, of being clothed in a parka—an inset of fur, or a line indicating trimming. Although there were a few deviations, the majority were made with the typically stylized Okvik face. Thule and late prehistoric figurines are almost indistinguishable. They are of two kinds, whole and half figures (Figs. 34, 39, 40). The former are characterized by their linearity, slight indications of sex, and their size. They are often quite large with carefully made arms and legs. The half figures have only a head and a bust, with no arms or sexual designations.

There is little doubt that most of these were made as dolls intended to be dressed in doll's clothing. Occasionally figures were jointed like marionettes or were provided with holes for suspension. Few of the excavated or collected ivory figures had holes, and scarcely any of them stand upright without support.

Although wooden dolls were made as toys, it appears that they were sometimes used for other purposes. A number of decorated wooden objects were used in connection with whaling and whaling ceremonies, but little is known about them. For instance, paddles were covered with many kinds of designs that represented both magical properties and ownership. Buckets to be used in whaling were thought to be more effective when decorated with ivory chains. In ceremonies that followed a successful whale hunt in the northern part of Seward Peninsula, a jointed man chased a jointed bear endlessly, but without getting anywhere.

Worked by strings from above, their legs ran furiously in the same spot.

The torso dolls might also have been used in whaling ceremonies,[2] but a number of them in museums have a soft body attached to the torso, indicating that they, too, were made only as playthings (Fig. 40).

The lifeless quality of Eskimo ivory dolls throughout the ages was the general rule; the faces usually reveal a careful consideration of the diagnostic points of the face, but no interpretation. One of the outstanding exceptions is the so-called "Okvik Madonna," a deeply patinated ivory figurine whose face is twisted into an enigmatic, almost cynical expression (Figs. 8, 9). Two other artists have also deviated from the unemotional tenor of the majority of the objects, one from St. Lawrence Island represented by a collection deposited in the University of Alaska Museum, and the other by a group in the American Museum of Natural History (Figs. 37, 38, 59-61). The former are fairly recent, of the 1920's, and closely resemble the Koryak wooden sculpture illustrated by Jochelson, not only in the surface details but also because they depict both action and emotion. These figures were supposed to have been given to women who were sterile.

The other examples are three wooden figurines collected in 1916 and given to the American Museum marked only with the provenience "Alaska." They appear to be the work of one man and bear a marked resemblance to the carved wooden figures from St. Lawrence Island. Undoubtedly all three of these are shamans' dolls intended to be used ceremonially, for they are equipped with holes and a thong for hanging. The knee of one of the figures is bent almost to the chin, the other leg made very straight. The pained expression of the face and the strained position of the body indicate both physical and mental struggle (Figs. 37, 38).

The very strange position of this climbing man points to one of those fascinating, but dangerous, relationships that inevitably appear when one searches for explanations. In this case, the speculation spans a distance of over three thousand miles and a chasm between oral literature and the more concrete form of carving. The Greenland Eskimos believed in a legendary cave dweller called Qivitoq who, though human in form,

[2]Otto William Geist and Froelich Rainey, *Archaeological Excavations at Kukulik* (Miscellaneous Publications of the University of Alaska, Vol. II; Washington, D.C.: Government Printing Office, 1936), Pl. 25, No. 21; Pl. 32, No. 8; Edward William Nelson, *The Eskimo about Bering Strait* (Bureau of American Ethnology, Annual Report, Vol. XVIII, Part I, 1899), Pl. XCIII, No. 8.

could fly by bending up one leg and stretching out the other exactly like the man in the Alaskan carving.[3]

A sculptural portrayal of human beings in action is clearly an innovation of the last century although activity of all kinds was represented on the nineteenth-century two-dimensional engraved ivory slabs and tusks. A number of bas-relief group sculptures of people, dog teams, houses, and ships, plainly European-inspired, have been preserved from the 1880's. These, in addition to the figurines from St. Lawrence and a few made at the present time at the suggestion of customers, are the only ones in the Bering Strait area that could be classified as "group sculpture." Their comparative costliness restricts sales, and the large amount of ivory needed for the figures and the base upon which they rest is a deterrent for the carvers with limited amounts of ivory.

In the contemporary period the concepts and goals of realism seem confined only to animals. One of the most important reasons for this is the change in carving human figures as a result of the influence of missionaries and educators, as discussed in chapter 7.

Animals, too, forfeited some of their former realistic features. For example, one of the carvers told me that the old Eskimo artists "used to put a hole under the tail of a fox or wolf, but the missionaries told them it was wrong so they stopped."

The carvers have made superb lifelike animals from the suggestions of persons who have been interested in the Eskimos' latent capabilities for naturalistic sculpture. Interpretation of musculature and characteristic attitudes have progressed to a distinctive peak. Unfortunately, there has been no opportunity for the carvers to do the same for the human figure because the missionary-inspired attitude toward nudity persists. There is every reason to believe that they could make exceptional human nudes, for, even though expressions were lacking and many of the ancient figures were quite uninteresting, many of the mid-nineteenth-century artists had carefully indicated back muscles and a groove down the back for the musculature over the spine. Unfortunately, when the occasion arises nowadays for making a nude figure, what is produced is usually a piece of eroticism ordered by a customer.

It is obvious that emotional interpretations have always been kept in

[3]Frederik Nielsen, "Greenland Culture," in *Greenland* (Ringkjøbing: Royal Danish Ministry for Foreign Affairs, ca. 1951), p. 69.

abeyance. It can be seen that naturalistic interpretation—that part which deals with the revelation of the emotions—is not considered realism by either ancient or modern carvers. Thus, none of the violence of the Eskimo's life is revealed in his carvings. Life today is still precarious, particularly among the carvers who live close to the old Eskimo way of life in the lonely outposts that are theirs alone for the greater part of a year. The hazards of hunting on the ice and water, and of battling the unpredictable arctic weather, are still manifold.

That their carvings show restraint from emotionalism and violence almost to the point of coldness is remarkable in view of other considerations also. For instance, many of the legends and "true" stories of the Eskimos contain threads of violence and cruelty, revenge, bodily harm including dismemberment, conflict situations,[4] and dwarfs, fabulous animals, and monsters. It might be argued that the present-day market is the restricting force in this respect, but we have seen that little archeological or even early historical art in this area was of an emotional or violent nature, so that the contemporary carving is only an extension of the earlier restraint. White culture has suggested most of the emotional content today.

In contrast to the frenzy by the Eskimos in some of their dances, the boundless effort they put forth in their athletic contests, and the heights of imagination they reach in their stories, it appears that their execution of exactness and precision is confined to matters of visual perception. Emotional and tactile perceptions have no limits as they see it. Interpretation of spatial relations, however, is limited to the sight, and, since carving is a visual pleasure rather than a tactile one, the same exactness and bounds that the Eskimo uses in measuring and interpreting his natural environment are used in this case. Instead of seeing chaos and indefinite, limitless space in their land of tundra and ice, as would a stranger, an Eskimo translates it into an orderly vista, and his relationship to it is precise and specific. This habit of reducing his environment to specific spatial relationships carries over into anything in which he feels the need for visual order.

For instance, aside from his carvings, all of his domestic and hunting tools and his transportation devices are neatly contrived. There is no

[4]Margaret Lantis, "Nunivak Eskimo Personality as Revealed in the Mythology," *Anthropological Papers of the University of Alaska*, II, No. 1 (1953), 113.

bursting out with nonessential details or parts. With his dancing and storytelling it is different. In these he is interpreting experience that cannot be reduced or perpetuated through the use of exact measurement, and in these the Bering Strait Eskimo has been more creative than in his carving. In neither of these does his interpretation have to satisfy the limitations of visual terms, for he is free to expand and interpolate beyond the bounds of visual measurement.

The carver himself is the severest critic of his carving, and it is only in the permanent form of ivory that the results of his creations can be viewed by him. A dance or story need not be attended by his constant self-judging in terms of volume, space, and linear relationships. Every good carver has his high standards, but he will never tell another person that he, himself, is a good carver, or that an object he has made is a fine piece. He may say, "That's the way I wanted to make it," or, "It is the best thing I ever did," but he will never judge his capabilities in comparison to those of others, or the merits of his own work in any terms except in comparison with his own standards.

TEN: The Artist: Past and Future

T HERE are indications that ivory carving, already two thousand years old, will remain a vital part of the Eskimos' lives as long as they continue to live on King and Little Diomede islands. There, as we have seen, ivory carving is a natural and inevitable part of living, and, although the younger generation may cast its lot with the "outside" world, there will always be some who will return to continue the tradition in its own milieu. Only when the Eskimos no longer live permanently on the islands will there be a change. It appears unlikely that such a step will occur voluntarily, at least if present conditions remain as they are. But we are constantly reminded today of both internal and external change in a land as unresistant and even hospitable to it as is Alaska. Any number of events could rob the islands of their inhabitants.

In order to maintain their identity with the Eskimo way of life, the islanders would have to settle on the mainland in a locality where they could continue to hunt sea animals. Otherwise they would have to revise their goals and accomplishments, and the change would affect their carving. Their walrus ivory supply would be virtually cut off, and their time consumed by the activities of earning a living. Probably a few, like those living permanently in Nome today, would continue to carve. For the most part, however, these are now the older men. The younger mainland Eskimos have taken easily to the more typically non-Eskimo patterns of living, including higher academic education and a livelihood derived from the fields of mechanics or business.

Ivory carving under such circumstances would either die out or continue as a pastime for the few, possibly fostered by an organization seeking to preserve "ancient" arts. In either case its place in the lives of the Eskimos would approach that of other cultures. It would cease to be the subtle, interpenetrating force that it is now and, presumably, always has been. There would be a dichotomy between the artist and nonartist, and the latter would become more numerous with the passage of time.

As it stands now, every Eskimo accepts the development of artistic talent as inevitable. The role of artist is not the unusual, or deviant, one. No man is faced with the problems of acceptance or rejection by other persons in his own group because of his decision to become an "artist," as is so often the case in the non-Eskimo world, but the creative talents of all of the men are brought to flower. The entire culture is much richer for this involvement in artistic activity that pervades the lives of all its people.

But although every Eskimo man can be called an artist according to white standards, even the best, as we have seen, will deny being one. This denial is not self-effacement, for he personally has the highest regard for his own talents and he knows that others do, too, but it is indicative of the ivory carver's position in both the Eskimo and non-Eskimo cultures of today. Although the Eskimos have successfully amalgamated portions of both cultures, they have refused parts of the new life and retained so tenaciously parts of their own that they appear to be in possession of two separately identifiable cultures. The artist needs no appreciation for his talents and no special recognition within his own culture because he is satisfying a creative drive that is the normal course of life.

For the non-Eskimo world the Eskimo artist is still cloaked in anonymity. He is first of all an Eskimo—unidentified. Actually, when "primitive" art is referred to as "anonymous" art, its anonymous character springs from the appraisal and, it might be said, the ignorance of the group that is discussing it. For the contemporary Eskimo artists, themselves, their art is no more anonymous than that of an artist in another culture who signs his work with letters six inches high, for every Eskimo artist's style is recognizable to everybody else, and every man's work is clearly distinguishable from that of anyone else.

Today, because he is still more oriented to the Eskimo culture where his status is already determined than to the non-Eskimo culture, the carver does not seek further individual recognition from the latter. The exceptions to this attitude have already been noted in chapter 3. He presents his art for sale as one of the members of a group, each of whom has already established his own individuality according to the standard of that group. Beyond this, he is concerned about his carvings as a part of the wares of the Eskimo group. Once he succeeds in these terms, nothing more matters for he has already found his way among his own people and has been accorded his individuality by them. He has the same feeling for himself and his coartists when confronted by the towering wall of the non-Eskimo world as he has for the polar bear skins stretched out for comparison and evaluation: "They're good; they're *all* good." Or he might be equally likely to say, "They're bad; they're *all* bad."

He is aware that the professional artist in non-Eskimo cultures often has a unique status, viewed with a number of reactions by the various segments of those societies. His own appraisal does not permit him to think of himself in similar terms because his training for his future artistry has been interwoven with all phases of his maturing. He grows up in our terms an artist, in his, a carver, the accepted and expected role that he will always play.

Appendix: Characteristic Motifs of Periods of Eskimo Carving

B EFORE the beginning of scientific archeological excavations in the Arctic thirty years ago, objects were dug up helter-skelter, here and there, usually with not so much as a word as to provenience or age except that they were "arctic" or "prehistoric." Moreover, the same confusion exists with the majority of historic Eskimo objects. Sometimes they are known to be "Eskimo" or come from "Alaska," the most specific labels bestowed upon them by many early collectors.

Private collections are more often in this bewildering state than those on public exhibition, but the latter are not exempt. Despite the apparent hopelessness of such an array of objects, however, it is now possible to add general identifying tags to the contents of the collections by employing a few diagnostic characteristics as guideposts.

The following word descriptions and diagrams of the various major Alaskan Eskimo art styles are of necessity simplified. Fuller information will be found in the following sources (for complete references see the Bibliography).

For archeology:

Henry B. Collins, Jr., *Archeology of St. Lawrence Island,* 1937.

Henry B. Collins, Jr., *Prehistoric Art of the Alaskan Eskimo,* 1929

Otto William Geist and Froelich Rainey, *Archaeological Excavations at Kukulik,* 1936.

J. L. Giddings, "The Archeology of Bering Strait," 1960.

Helge Larsen and Froelich Rainey, *Ipiutak and the Arctic Whale Hunting Culture,* 1948.

Froelich G. Rainey, *Eskimo Prehistory: The Okvik Site on the Punuk Islands,*
1941.

For nineteenth-century and contemporary art:
Hans Himmelheber, *Eskimokünstler,* 1938.
Walter James Hoffman, *The Graphic Art of the Eskimos,* 1897.

The inadequacies of conveying a style of art through line drawings
should be pointed out here. In some cases the same components of design
have been employed in various times and areas, and it is only in the
actual execution of them on ivory that differences are readily apparent.
For example, the Y element is used by both early historic and Okvik
artists, but the former used it primly and stiffly, and the latter in a freehand, almost careless manner. For the truest picture, therefore, the diagrams should be used in conjunction with photographs. Only incised
surface decoration is illustrated in the line drawings; other information
is more readily gained from the text or photographs.

The smallest units of design are here designated "components," the
larger ones, "designs." This more or less an arbitrary terminology should
help to eliminate confusion. The Birnirk art, which is not yet well defined
but has resemblances to Old Bering Sea and Amur River art (Siberia),
and several other site styles have been omitted in this general account.

OKVIK PERIOD

Human figurines are found in abundance. They are usually female,
linear in body and face, with long noses, small pointed chins, small
mouths, incised eyebrows, and sometimes tattoo marks on the face (Figs.
10-12). The bodies often have incised clothing designs. The Okvik artist
decorated numerous harpoon heads and unidentified objects, and, except
for one class of harpoon heads, the incisions are light, shallow, and "lacy."
The entire object was used for one integrated design with usually only
one central point of interest (Figs. 14-16, 109).

The principal components used were long and short parallel lines,
spurred lines, disconnected lines, wedges, and the Y figure (see Fig. 108).
Occasionally used were a ladderlike figure (hereafter called a ladder
line), rows of dots, circles, and the circle-dot (also called the nucleated
circle). The disconnected lines in a row were not used in close conjunction with solid lines as in the Old Bering Sea period that followed, but

were spaced equidistant between them. There were several extremely subtle styles in this period that are confusing enough to worry the archeologists for some time to come.

THE OLD BERING SEA PERIOD

The Old Bering Sea artist conceived many units and focal points on his objects. Many of the components described above as Okvik were called Old Bering Sea I by Collins, and those we include here were called Old Bering Sea II and III. There are actually two definite styles of Old Bering Sea: the very ornate, complicated style pictured in Figure 22 and on the right in Figure 20, which will be called Classic Old Bering Sea here, and the simpler kind exemplified by Figure 20 (left) and in the harpoon head on the right in Figure 19.

The most commonly used components (Fig. 108) were parallel lines, broken lines, double circles, the ladder line, and a wedge combined with a circle. Less often used were a plus sign or cross, short parallel lines enclosed by an outline, and several kinds of spurred lines. The last, when used, are bold. The centers of ovals or "eyes" in the Classic Old Bering Sea were often raised into bosses, sometimes with inlays inserted into them.

PUNUK PERIOD

The art of the Punuk period is usually simpler in concept and more rigid and angular in design than Okvik or Old Bering Sea. Design units are more likely to be made up of short straight lines and compass-made circles or nucleated circles. Punuk art has been called "stiff and degenerate" because of its simplicity, following as it does upon the heels of the complex Classic Old Bering Sea style. It is nevertheless disarmingly pleasing and beautifully conceived. The compass-made nucleated circle was supposedly used only by the later Punuk people; but whether or not this is true remains to be seen, for there are no freehand circles of any kind in the Punuk period. The spurred line was utilized, the spurs often terminating with dots. Whereas alternating spurs were rarely found in Okvik, and never in Old Bering Sea, they were used lavishly in Punuk. The broken lines of Old Bering Sea and the dash-dash fill-ins of Okvik are absent. The Punuk artists used a decisive hand; they were precise and particular craftsmen. The principal components (Figs. 110, 111) were the ladder line, many parallel lines, spurred lines of various kinds, dots, the nucleated circle, and an enclosed triangular figure. Punuk objects are illustrated in Figures 23-27.

IPIUTAK

Ipiutak art represents some of the most unusual forms found so far in archeological sites (Figs. 29-32). There are numerous openwork carvings of ivory; many associated with swivels, ivory chain links, and animal carvings in the Scytho-Siberian tradition; and decorated browbands. The Scytho-Siberian style is reflected in the use of fantastic heads as terminal objects, skeletal outlines on the exterior of animals, raised bosses (as in Old Bering Sea), and inlays.

The strange thing about Ipiutak art is that only when all of the art is observed does any specific "Ipiutak" art style emerge. Only a few individual objects—masks, browbands, and a few unidentified objects— can be said to be in the "Ipiutak style." The remainder are reminiscent of Old Bering Sea and Okvik. There are, however, a few components of surface decoration that are different from other periods. A characteristic one is the use of a dark and a light line together to form longitudinal parallel lines. Whereas the Old Bering Sea artist faced a light line with broken lines, the Ipiutak artist faced a dark line with a light line. He also used many kidney-shaped, oval, and round outlines, often enclosing other designs; the circle-dot; various kinds of Y; a few broken lines or dots; jet inlays; and a ladder line on animals (Figs. 110, 111).

THULE AND LATE PREHISTORIC PERIODS

The Thule and late prehistoric periods in Alaska were richer in sculptured animals, flat-bottomed birds, and figurines than in geometric ornamentation. The characteristics of the simple but effective sculpture can be identified more readily from Figures 27-33 than through description. The sculpture was lineal in concept. The animals often have sagging stomachs, stumpy legs, and elongated necks. Many ivory objects were undecorated; when they were decorated, the ornamentation was usually only in borders. The artists used few components: the Y figure, single and double spurred line, a few parallel lines. Rows of dots were often drilled on the tops of birds.

NINETEENTH CENTURY

The northern nineteenth-century Eskimos produced figurines like those shown in Figures 34 and 35, using very little more imagination in their geometric ornamentation than their predecessors. But these were the artists who developed the forceful representational engravings on ivory (Figs. 44-52), probably as an indirect result of an abundance of steel engraving tools. To a small degree they also painted on wood, as realistically as they engraved on ivory.

These artists gave a great deal of attention to details of finish on their sculptured animals, putting insets of baleen or ivory into the eyes, ears, and anus. The principal components used were the raised spurred line (zigzag), a heavy spurred line, nucleated circle, parallel lines, the Y figure, and a trident (Fig. 112).

The southwest Alaskan artist at this time carved very few human or animal ivory figurines and made few realistic life sketches on ivory. His talents in that direction were diverted to painting mythical and fantastic figures on ceremonial paraphernalia including spoons and drumtops (see Fig. 43). The ornamentation on such ivory objects as buttons, needlecases, handles, and so forth was usually lavish. It is these designs which are illustrated in Figures 41, 42, and 112. The carver used many geometric designs, the most common of which are presented here. The most popular components were the oblique spurred line in many variations, crosshatching, a V figure, the ladder line, the Y figure, many parallel lines, and the nucleated circle, often with many concentric circles and spurs.

When the southwest Alaskan Eskimo carved dolls—often of wood— the faces were flat and round with upturned or downturned mouth, in contrast to the northern cylindrical face with usually only a gash for a mouth (Figs. 34, 39, 40).

The settlement of St. Michael appears to have been the meeting place for the southern and northern art styles, mainly because of its role in historic times as a trading center. The most common use of the two styles together was on the large ivory pipes, which were often decorated both with the geometric designs of the Southwest and the realistic life sketches of the North.

Bibliography

Antropova, V.V. "Bone Carving of the Present Day Eskimo and Chukchee," *Akademiia Nauk,* Muzei Antropologi, Sbornik, XV (1953), 5-122. In Russian.

Ashley, Clifford W. *The Yankee Whaler.* New York: Houghton Mifflin Co., 1926.

Beechey, F.W. *Narrative of a Voyage to the Pacific and Beering's Strait, 1825-1828.* London, 1831.

Bishop Museum. *Hawaiian Collections.* Handbook, Part I, 1915.

Burns, Cecil K. "A Monograph on Ivory Carving," *The Journal of Indian Art and Industry,* IX, No. 75 (1901), 53-56.

Cammann, Schuyler. "Carvings in Walrus Ivory," *University Museum Bulletin,* The University Museum, University of Pennsylvania, Philadelphia, Vol. XVIII, No. 3 (1954).

Chard, Chester S. "Eskimo Archaeology in Siberia," *Southwestern Journal of Anthropology,* XI (1955), 150-77.

Collins, Henry B., Jr., *Archeology of St. Lawrence Island.* Smithsonian Miscellaneous Collections, Vol. XCVI, No. 1, 1937.

———. *Arctic Area—Indigenous Period.* Programa de historia de America. Mexico City: Instituto panamericano de geografia e historia, 1954.

———. "The Origin and Antiquity of the Eskimo," *Smithsonian Institution Report 1950,* pp. 423-67, Washington, D.C.: Government Printing Office, 1951.

———. "Outline of Eskimo Prehistory," in *Essays in Historical Anthropology of North America,* pp. 533-92. Smithsonian Miscellaneous Collections, Vol. C, 1940.

————. *Prehistoric Art of the Alaskan Eskimo.* Smithsonian Miscellaneous Collections, Vol. LXXXI, No. 4, 1929.

Cook, John A. *Pursuing the Whale.* New York: Houghton Mifflin Co., 1926.

Curtis, Edward S. *The North American Indian,* Vol. XX. Norwood, Mass., 1930.

Department of Northern Affairs and National Resources, Canada. *Canadian Eskimo Art.* Ottawa, 1957.

Geist, Otto, and Froelich Rainey. *Archaeological Excavations at Kukulik.* Miscellaneous Publications of the University of Alaska, Vol. II. Washington, D.C.: Government Printing Office, 1936.

Giddings, J.L. "The Archeology of Bering Strait," *Current Anthropology,* I, No. 2 (March, 1960), 121-37, with comments by Chester S. Chard, Henry B. Collins, David M. Hopkins, Helge Larsen, and M.G. Levin.

Harrison, E.S. *Nome and the Seward Peninsula.* Seattle, 1905.

Heinrich, Albert, "Some Present-Day Acculturative Innovations in a Non-literate Society," *American Anthropologist,* LII, No. 2 (1950), 235-42.

Himmelheber, Hans. *Eskimokünstler.* Stuttgart: Strecker and Schröder, 1938.

Hoffman, Walter James. *The Graphic Art of the Eskimos.* U.S. National Museum, Annual Report for 1895, pp. 739-968. Washington, D.C., 1897.

Holtved, Erik. "Archaeological Investigations in the Thule District," *Meddelelser om Grønland,* Vol. CXLI, Part II (1944).

Hrdlička, Aleš. *Anthropological Survey in Alaska.* Bureau of American Ethnology, Annual Report 46, 1930.

Jochelson, Vladimir Ilich. *The Koryak.* Memoirs of the American Museum of Natural History, Vol. X, 1905-6.

Keithahn, Edward L. *Igloo Tales* (with illustrations by George Aden Ahgupuk). Education Division, U.S. Indian Service. Lawrence, Kans.: Haskell Institute, 1945.

Lantis, Margaret. "Nunivak Eskimo Personality as Revealed in the Mythology," *Anthropological Papers of the University of Alaska,* II, No. 1 (1953), 109-74.

Larsen, Helge, and Froelich Rainey. *Ipiutak and the Arctic Whale Hunting Culture.* Anthropological Papers, American Museum of Natural History, Vol. XLII, 1948.

Mason, J. Alden. "Eskimo Pictorial Art," *The Museum Journal,* The Museum of the University of Pennsylvania, Philadelphia, XVIII, No. 3 (1927), 248-83.

Mathiassen, Therkel. "Ancient Eskimo Settlements in the Kangamiut Area," *Meddelelser om Grønland,* XCI (1931), 1-150.

————.*Archaeology of the Central Eskimos.* Report of the Fifth Thule Expedition, Vol. IV, Parts I and II, 1927.

————. *Report on the Expedition*. Report of the Fifth Thule Expedition, Vol. I, Part I, 1945.

Nelson, Edward William. *The Eskimo about Bering Strait*. Bureau of American Ethnology, Annual Report, Vol. XVIII, Part I, 1899.

Nielsen, Frederik. "Greenland Culture," in *Greenland*. Ringkjøbing: Royal Danish Ministry for Foreign Affairs, ca. 1951.

Nordenskiöld, A.E. *The Voyage of the Vega round Asia and Europe*. New York: Macmillan and Co., 1882.

Rainey, Froelich G. *Eskimo Prehistory: The Okvik Site on the Punuk Islands*. Anthropological Papers, American Museum of Natural History, Vol. XXXVII, Part IV, 1941.

————, and Elizabeth Ralph. "Radiocarbon Dating in the Arctic," *American Antiquity*, XXIV, No. 4 (1959), 365-74.

Rasmussen, Knud. *The Western Alaska Eskimo*. Posthumous notes edited by Erik Holtved and H. Ostermann. Report of the Fifth Thule Expedition, Vol. X, No. 3, 1952.

Ray, Dorothy Jean. "Alaska's Billikens—Bits of Good Luck in Ivory," *The Seattle Sunday Times Magazine*, May 26, 1957, p. 7.

————."The Ivory Carvers," *Alaska Sportsman*, Statehood Issue, XXV, No. 6 (June, 1959), 26-29, 80-81. Reprinted in *The Alaska Book*. Chicago: J. G. Ferguson Publishing Co., 1960, pp. 258-62.

————. "Where Every Man's an Artist," *The Seattle Sunday Times Magazine*, April 13, 1958, p. 3.

————."The Mystery of the Billiken," *Alaska Sportsman*, XXVI, No. 9 (September, 1960), 36-37, 56.

VanStone, James W. "Carved Human Figures from St. Lawrence Island, Alaska," *Anthropological Papers of the University of Alaska*, Vol. 2, No. 1, 1953, pp. 19-29.

Zagoskin, L. A. Account of Pedestrian Journeys in the Russian Possessions in America in 1842, 1843, and 1844 (1847). Translated into English by Mrs. Antoinette Hotovitzky. Typewritten MS, Library of Congress Card No. F907.Z182.

————. *Lieutenant Zagoskin's Travels in Russian America, 1842-1844*. Translated by Penelope Rainey. Edited by Henry N. Michael. Toronto: University of Toronto Press, 1967. (Translation of 1956 edition)

Index